Michael Bublé

THE BIOGRAPHY

Juliet Peel

piatkus

PIATKUS

First published in Great Britain in 2009 by Piatkus
This paperback edition published in 2010 by Piatkus

Copyright © 2009 by Juliet Peel

The moral right of the author has been asserted.

A CIP catalogue record for this book
is available from the British Library.

ISBN 978-0-7499-4143-7

Typeset in Bembo by M Rules
Printed and bound in Great Britain by
Clays Ltd, St Ives plc

Papers used by Piatkus are natural, renewable and
recyclable products sourced from well-managed forests and certified
in accordance with the rules of the Forest Stewardship Council.

Mixed Sources
Product group from well-managed
forests and other controlled sources
www.fsc.org Cert no. SGS-COC-004081
© 1996 Forest Stewardship Council

FSC

Piatkus
An imprint of
Little, Brown Book Group
100 Victoria Embankment
London EC4Y 0DY

An Hachette UK Company
www.hachette.co.uk

www.piatkus.co.uk

Contents

1

Sunshine – Learn Al Martino Before I Die

It was a mellow day in Burnaby, a suburb of Vancouver in British Columbia, and the Bublé family was wildly excited. Lewis Bublé, a fisherman, and his wife Amber, were about to witness the arrival of their first child, and on 9 September 1975, Michael Steven Bublé made his appearance on the world stage. Michael was to appear on many, many other stages in later life, but at the time there was nothing to give any indication that Amber had given birth to a son who was to become an internationally acclaimed star, for the Bublés were from a humble, working-class background. Originally a family of Italian immigrants, life back then was about survival: work, keeping a roof over your head and raising a family. Lewis and Amber were to have two more children, Brandee and Crystal – who went on to become an actress – but it was their eldest who was to make the biggest name for himself. A star really had been born.

There had been no history of show business in the Bublé

family: no indication at all as to what was to be. And life was hard. Lewis, who fished salmon, spent the summers out on his boat, working to look after his family. The days were long, the water freezing, and the kind of luxury Michael was to experience in later years was just a dream. It was a blue-collar life: Michael's maternal grandfather Mitch Santaga, who was to have a huge influence on his life, was a plumber, albeit one who adored swing music, a passion he was to pass on to his grandson to enormous effect. For a man who was to inherit the mantle of the great crooners, Michael's background could not have been more down to earth. This was an immigrant family who had come to Canada to find the good life. Although they'd had no real hardship to endure, they certainly hadn't found that life yet.

Where did it come from, though, this performing gene? Not from his parents, that was for sure. Indeed, when he was still a young kid, Michael looked almost certain to follow in his father's footsteps. 'My dad is a fisherman, his dad was a fisherman – hell, I was a fisherman,' Michael volunteered in the early days, when people finally started to take notice of him. There was nothing whatsoever starry or showbiz in Michael's life – except for the music so loved by his grandpa Mitch. 'We were never dirt poor,' Michael recalled. 'We got Christmas presents and stuff. We were middle class – nice people. But of course we had to worry – still do – about money.' His parents certainly did: they had three children to raise and Lewis worked in a precarious industry. But somehow they managed to get by. The most important thing was family – as long as they all had one another, they would pull ahead. And for all the unlikelihood of Michael coming from such a background, that sense of security in his family was to prove enormously important in the years to come. First there was to be his long, drawn out apprenticeship, then times when he lost his way and finally some considerable degree of heartbreak on Michael's part. But his family was always there.

Michael himself had been born with the music gene, however, and that became obvious when he was barely out of nappies. He was a showman from very early on. An exceptionally lively child, Michael was always fooling around, singing, dancing and drawing attention to himself. 'You were always performing since you were two in front of the fire-place,' Amber told her son in an interview the two of them did together many years later, after he'd become famous. 'You were Gene Gene the Dancing Machine. He told us when he was really young, "I'm different. You'll see. When I'm older I'm going to be really famous." You knew.'

There is always a temptation, if not to rewrite the past, at least to decorate it, and if truth be told, it was not until he was in his teens that it began to become apparent that Michael had an exceptional voice. But that love of music was implanted very early on. As far as he can recall, it began in earnest at the tender age of four. Michael heard Bing Crosby singing 'White Christmas', and that was it: he was hooked. Perhaps it was fortunate that it was Bing who was his formative influence rather than, say, the Sex Pistols, for that is exactly the style of music he has made his own. 'Those swinging arrangements,' he recalled of that moment when he first heard Bing sing. 'I thought, "Wow, this is great." Even now, I can sing you any sax line from that record.' There are various accounts of who played him the music, but it might well have been Mitch, who certainly introduced his grandson to many other of Bing's fellow crooners as time went by. And the music took hold from a very early age. Michael's love of the type of songs he sings stretches right back into his earliest childhood. If truth be told, he was never going to sign up to any other type of musical style.

But there was personality involved, too. Backing up Amber's account, Michael recalls displaying determination from an extremely early age. By the time he was six, he was certain what he wanted to do. 'I said, "I'm different. I'm going to play shows all over the world,"' he once explained. 'I had this burning inside me right from the start. Sometimes I wonder if maybe something was missing inside me, because why should I burn so badly, why should I be so driven? When most kids wanted to be firemen, how come I knew exactly what I would be? Now my mother thinks it's very strange; it gives her the heebie jeebies.' Back then, however, she was not so convinced. 'They said, "That's nice, honey, but we'll love you no matter what . . ."'

It was a telling observation on Michael's part: why did he feel so different from other kids his age? One easy answer, and one that might account for his subsequent success, is that he was different from those other kids. Seeing him up on stage today, relaxed, easy-going and oozing confidence, it is very difficult to imagine Michael Bublé as anything other than a regular guy, one who is very popular with the ladies, who enjoys going for a beer after work. But back then he didn't quite fit in, and it might well have been a sense of isolation that gave him a concentration and a determination to succeed in later life.

Certainly, the musicality was always there. As a child, Michael learnt his address by singing it: 'Three Oh Four Eight, Car-din-al Drive.' And, as his father was away for long periods on the boat, Michael developed a preternaturally close relationship with his grandpa Mitch – aka Demetrio Santaga, originally from the village of Preganziol, about 40 kilometres from Padua. Grandpa loved the old songs, many of them sung by the children of Italian immigrants, and Michael grew to love them, too. As a good Italian, of course, Mitch adored the likes of Frank Sinatra and Dean Martin – but he loved the rest of them, as well. Would Michael have developed in the way he did if he didn't have Grandpa Mitch constantly egging him on? It's impossible to say.

But the fact that Lewis was away so much on the boat did mean that Michael saw far more of his grandparents than he might have been expected to, under other circumstances. Grandpa and Grandma looked after the girls, too. But it was Michael who shared Mitch's love of music, and a particularly strong bond developed between them. 'Michael's dad wasn't around in the summertime, so the kids would come over all the time,' Mitch's wife Yolanda, Michael's grandmother, would later recall.

'To please his grandfather, Michael would learn all these old songs. But he loved them, too, and it seemed like he would hear a song once and be able to sing it.' That certainly was an innate talent. Mitch might have introduced him to the music, but only something he was born with would have allowed him to have that almost instant recall.

But that was only the half of it. Mitch had a particular way of getting Michael to learn the songs. 'My grandfather would always say, "Sunshine," – that's his nickname for me – "learn Al Martino before I die,"' Michael recalled. '"Learn the Mills Brothers. Louis Prima." I'd feel guilty so I'd listen and learn.' It was a strategy that worked: it is often said that after he started out, Michael took eight years to become an overnight success. The reality was that it took much longer. He'd been practising since he was a young child.

Mitch's influence cannot be overstated. That early exposure to Bing Crosby might have alerted Michael to a whole other world out there, but it was Mitch who developed his tastes, nurtured him and introduced him to the singers he himself knew and loved so well. Michael listened to all the modern greats: Ella Fitzgerald, Rosemary Clooney, Bobby Darin and Elvis (who Michael was later to play in a musical), to name but a few.

'My grandfather was really my best friend growing up,' Michael said. 'He was the one who opened me up to a whole world of music that seemed to have been passed over by my generation. Although I like rock 'n' roll and modern music, the first time my grandad played me the Mills Brothers, some-thing magical happened. The lyrics were so romantic, so real . . . the way a song should be for me. It was like seeing my future flash before me. I wanted to be a singer and I knew that this was the music that I wanted to sing. I was always taken by this style. Listening to Mel Tormé or Ella Fitzgerald or Frank Sinatra as a kid was so great because they had this dulcet tonal quality that I hadn't heard in modern singers. I would hear a swing tune on the soundtrack to a film or on an advertise-ment, and I didn't know when it was written or who was playing it but, man, I knew that I liked it.'

That total immersion when he was still so young was to stand Michael in extremely good stead. He grew used to hearing the way other singers played with the music, the words, the melodies. No two versions of one song were ever exactly the same, and so he began to understand that a singer interprets the lyrics, makes them his own. He also began to see the songs as treasures, masterpieces to hand down the generations. When he was still a young child, many of the great crooners of the old days were still alive, but by the time he'd taken to the stage himself, most of them had gone. He developed a sense of wanting to preserve something beautiful: something that could die out were people like Michael not around to bring it back to life. That sense remains with him to this day.

But family was quite as important as music and Michael was also very close to his parents. Because Amber had been so very young when she'd had Michael, only twenty, the relationship sometimes seemed more akin to brother and sister, especially as Amber would let him get away with behaviour most mothers would condemn. Indeed, she positively encouraged it. Many years later, when the two of them gave a joint interview, Michael recalled his unusual schooldays, spent first at Seaforth Elementary and then at Cariboo Hill Secondary. 'She would come during class and pull me out,' he said. 'All the kids would watch, thinking I had to go to the dentist, and she'd take me to McDonald's. She was my mom, but also my friend.'

Back in the very early years of his childhood, Michael had a happy and secure existence. Family life was warm and his time at school went well. He looks back on those years with nostalgia: 'I loved my time at Seaforth Elementary in Burnaby, Canada, which was a school that parents fought to get their kids into,' he recalled in an interview given when he'd become an international star. 'It was a wonderful, sheltered, cosy place with great teachers and a principal who knew everyone's name. My sixth- and seventh-grade teacher was Mrs Moore, and I had a huge crush on her. She was a strikingly beautiful woman, about thirty at the time. She was an amazing person. At that age it had an effect on me, to see a woman who was so gorgeous but strong, too. She was quite reserved, very classy, and I'd do anything to give Mrs Moore an apple.'

Here was an early appreciation of the female form, all quite properly expressed, too. But it was not just the fact that Mrs Moore was an attractive woman that made an impact on him: it was the attitude of the teachers that cheered him on, as well. Utterly committed to bringing the pupils on, the staff at the school created an atmosphere in which the children thrived, something that Michael would not always find as he moved on to his teenage years. 'At Seaforth, it was noticeable that all the teachers really cared,' he recalled. 'I realised that I had people pushing me along, fostering me. But high school was a completely different world.'

For Michael's precociousness as a performer was beginning to set him increasingly apart. For a start, his taste in music was totally different from that of the other kids: swing rather than rock. It couldn't help but make him stand out from the crowd, which is not always what a teenager wants. The urge to conform is extremely strong and Michael didn't. Back then, as he occasionally admits, he was seen as something of a geek.

Michael, citing Mitch as his influence, professed not to care. 'When I was twelve, he played me Vic Damone's version of "It Had to Be You" and I told him that it was great, so he started making me tapes from his old records,' he explained. 'For the first time I was hearing Al Martino and the Mills Brothers, and I would be learning ten of these songs a day by heart because I loved them so much. See, I always had a bad attitude towards conforming and I never wanted to be trendy, so I couldn't give a shit about what everyone at school was into.'

That was a defiant attitude established when Michael was well into the stardom years, and perhaps loath to admit to early vulnerability. But at other times, he admitted that it was tough. In an interview given in 2003, when he had only just hit the big time, his tone was somewhat different. He was not, he admitted, a popular schoolboy. He certainly wasn't the sought-after ladies' man he was to become in later years. 'I was a little chubby,' he said. 'I was the sweet kid. I was nice. Kids are all afraid and when they see someone who is weak . . . By the time I got out of high school I was a fighter.'

In other words, by this time he was bullied, or at least, knocked about. His drive, determination and work ethic were beginning to make him stand out from the crowd, too: unlike many of his peers, he not only had a sense that he wanted to make it, but he knew exactly how he wanted to make it. Some of the most successful people in the world had troubled childhoods – indeed, many psychologists believe that difficult early years can often propel people into spending the rest of their lives proving themselves against all the odds – and so it was coming to be with Michael. The popular kids behaved in one way and liked a particular type of music. Michael had more individual tastes and didn't go along with the crowd.

Not that he was really aware of why it was happening at the time. Why did he stand apart? he was asked. 'For not being loud,' Michael told an interviewer, clearly trying to understand it in retrospect himself. 'No, for being – I don't know. I'm still trying to figure it out. I was a little dork. I would pretend to listen to other music than what I was listening to, so at the water cooler I would go, "Oh yeah, yeah, I love that Run-DMC song!" "You don't know it!" "Yes I do!"'

It was no coincidence at all that at exactly the time Michael began to find school life difficult, his singing voice was beginning to stand out. Even taking into account that this was the partisan opinion of a family member, Grandpa Mitch was beginning to realise that this might be considerably more than a hobby. The kid was good. Really good. 'He used to sing with a broom handle as a mike,' Mitch recalled. 'He was a born performer, a real hambone. Then, one Boxing Day, when he was about fourteen, he started singing "New York, New York" with a karaoke set he got for Christmas. He floored me. I thought, "This guy's really got talent."'

He did, but it didn't help matters at school. 'At Cariboo Hill Secondary School, I sometimes felt a little alone,' he later confessed. 'I suppose I was an eccentric kid. I loved acting and music. I wasn't part of the hip crowd and I felt pressure to fit in. At times it was hard for me, but I enjoyed classes and I loved meeting girls. I also loved to sing and I'd often perform spontaneously in the cafeteria at lunchtime. I even delivered singing telegrams, to raise money for the school. When I think about it now, how embarrassing does that sound? But it was sweet and fun to do.'

It might have been, but it was not typical behaviour for a teenage boy and would hardly have endeared him to his peers. And, of course, it became a circle. The more Michael stood out in ways he didn't want to, the more he took refuge in his music, and the more he took refuge in his music, the more he stood out in ways he didn't want to. All the bravado in the world couldn't change that.

Not all his tastes were so different from his peers: he liked what was for his fellow students the more mainstream stuff, too. Even then, however, he still felt it couldn't match the stuff he knew best. 'I thought Kurt Cobain was a great writer,' Michael told one interviewer in 2004. 'It was the first time I had heard anything in this vein, and I don't think I wanted to like it – it was too angry, too cool – but it had good songs. This is the kind of thing that kids at school were listening to but I wonder, if they were given the opportunity and they weren't so worried about following each other, whether they wouldn't listen to Mel Tormé instead.'

He was also a big fan of George Michael, to whom, in voice terms, he has sometimes been compared, in particular the song 'Faith'. 'I couldn't give a shit if he's gay or straight or he does it with animals,' Michael continued. 'This guy makes good music. Almost every song on here [the *Faith* album] is top-notch, and this record made a big impression on me when I was thirteen or fourteen. I remember dancing to "Kissing a Fool" with this girl that I really liked. How can anyone not enjoy that song? But that's why there are thirty-one flavours of ice cream, eh?'

On another occasion, Michael remarked that he was glad not to be one of the sheep following the herd and developing a slavish devotion to the likes of Jon Bon Jovi, as the rest of his classmates did. But, for all those spontaneous performances in the canteen, the knowledge that he was not like his peers in some ways would have taken its toll. Nor did it help that he wasn't an outstanding student – or outstanding anything else more obviously school-oriented – which would, at the very least, have given him some way in which to fit in. He adored ice hockey – the sport often referred to in North America simply as 'hockey' – but he wasn't good enough to stand out there and be a jock, either. Only his music made him stand out.

'I was an average student – my attention span was pretty short,' Michael recalled of those teen years. 'I didn't always feel challenged, and I would get bored easily. I enjoyed English and social studies, but I just couldn't understand math. Having said that, my favourite teacher was my tenth-grade math teacher, Mr Clarke. He started every class with a puzzle based on linear thinking. I wasn't very good, but I would always try hard and I sensed he was aware of that. He appreciated the amount of effort I put in. And he didn't fail me; I guess he realised that wouldn't send the right message to myself or others who were struggling. I missed Mr Clarke when he got sick and didn't come back to school. I was crushed. He was the only one who made maths fun.'

He was, however, increasingly beginning to develop that love of ice hockey that stays with him to this day. It was one of the few things he had in common with his fellow students, and allowed him a rush, a physical surge of adrenalin that helped to cope with any feelings of alienation he might have had. By his own telling of it, he would rather have been a professional hockey player than a crooner: 'I wanted so bad to be a hockey player and the truth is that I sucked,' he confessed to an interviewer years later. 'If I was any good at hockey I probably wouldn't be singing right now. I'd probably be sitting out the season.'

In truth, by far the greatest influences on Michael's life were out of school altogether: Lewis and Mitch. Michael had a phenomenally close relationship with both of them, and in the latter case, was able to develop the interests that were going to pave his career in later life. Any sense of not belonging in the school playground was entirely dissipated in the warmth of home: in the bosom of a close family who adored each other and cheered each other on, Michael came into his own. That unquestioning support was to stand him in good stead in later years, providing him with a comfort blanket of absolute security, and it was something Michael has acknowledged to this day.

'My greatest teachers were my father and grandfather,' he said in an interview in his early thirties. 'They are extraordinary men who have achieved everything with integrity and honour. They taught me by their example and made me who I am. My grandfather also influenced me musically. We would sit for hours listening to music and arguing about who was the best singer or the best arranger. It was our common ground and I guess we bonded. Even today – he's eighty years old, I'm thirty-two – we're still best friends.'

The family kept him grounded, too. When Michael first achieved mega-success, it rather went to his head, turning him, as he admitted himself, into a jerk. His family was one of the elements that turned him back again. He knew he could trust them because they'd been there for him all his life: as a teenager when he felt alienated, and as a young man in his twenties, when he repeatedly failed to make the big time before finally pulling through. The very essence of Michael can be found in the relationship with his family: it defines him as much as his music does.

Nor did Michael sever his ties with his old neighbourhood once he had finally achieved fame. He was a small-town boy from Canada, and he never lost sight of that fact. But he certainly outgrew the old neighbourhood, whether he wanted to or not: while so many of the people he was at school with went on to become blue-collar workers, Michael became an international success. It took some time for that to sink in for both Michael and everyone else.

Indeed, he was to experience one of the odder consequences of enormous success: that the people he had grown up with now viewed him in a totally different light, so much so that it was he who had, to put it bluntly, the power, and not them. For a non-academic boy who left school when he was still very young and who took the best part of a decade to make it after that, the thrill must have been sweet indeed, once Michael had discovered that the tables had totally turned.

But they turned in ways that unnerved him, too. 'I keep in touch with my old elementary school and I like to help them out,' he said, at the age of thirty-two. 'I've become friends with the teachers, but the dynamics are strange now – I still see them as larger-than-life figures. I ran into Mrs Moore while I was at the school some months ago to present a cheque and she was visibly nervous when speaking to me. I couldn't get over it. I thought: "Please don't be nervous. I'm the one who should be nervous talking to you – you're Mrs Moore!" And, by the way, she's still beautiful.' The Bublé charm was as strong as ever; what Mrs Moore made of it all has not been revealed.

There was also a reconciliation, if you can call it that, with Cariboo Hill. In 2005, when Michael had become far and away its most famous ex-pupil, he clearly had forgiven and forgotten any unhappiness he might ever have experienced there, and decided to give the school something to make the link between alma mater and pupil clear. His father Lewis thus presented the institution with a plaque featuring a copy of his first mega-selling album *Michael Bublé*, along with sales accreditation seals. On top of that, the Cariboo Hill Grad Fashion Show featured some of Michael's songs. Both school and pupil revelled in the connection now.

Michael has been too tactful, in public, at least, to say what he thought of the fellow students who didn't always make his life so easy back then. But he has never tried to hide how much he loves his fame. There are so many stars out there who complain bitterly about the pressures of success but, perhaps in part because of his childhood, Michael has never been one of them. He knew how lucky he was; he wasn't going to pretend otherwise.

But also in contrast to his sometimes laddish image, Michael had a far more spiritual side than was at first apparent. As was to be expected of an Italian immigrant family, the Bublés were good Catholics, and Michael was brought up within the church. His upbringing was devout and traditional, although he did begin to develop a personal attitude towards it as time went on, one that he holds to this day.

'I'd say that I have a good personal relationship with Christ,' he told one interviewer. '[But] you know, we were going to these churches that were more opulent than any hotel I'd ever been in, and I was thinking, "Now, there are poor people and sick people and much as I love God's house to look good, this is ridiculous." I didn't like the fact that you can't talk to God when you need to forgive your sins – you have to go through this man – and I just thought, "That doesn't fit." I didn't like the fact that if you were gay, you were . . .' His voice trailed off.

As he got a little older, Michael also began to realise there were other advantages to a mellifluous singing voice. Much later in life, he joked he only became a singer to get laid; back then, however, he was beginning to realise that his talents certainly made him more attractive to the opposite sex. A clue came when he saw a picture of Harry Connick Jr in the locker of one of the popular teenage beauties at school: it was covered with lipstick kisses. 'I thought for the first time, "Maybe I could get girls out of this,"' he relates. He was fifteen at the time. But it was to be quite a while before Michael became a heartthrob: the girls back then were still more likely to be going out with jocks.

Michael was also becoming aware that there might be another, very good reason to pursue a singing career: the alternative was to live as hard a life as his father had always done. Ever since he entered his teens, Lewis had been taking him out on the boat in the summer, and Michael was beginning to realise that this was extremely hard work. The hours were long, the weather (and water) often freezing and the rewards were not that great. 'Man, it was hard,' Michael recalled. 'We'd be outside, four a.m., pouring rain. I'd be sitting there, freezing cold, tired, just dying. I'd cry and say to my dad, "You asshole, how could you make your son come out here?" I was terrified I'd have to work like he did.'

But it gave him a strong work ethic, one which was to remain with him from that moment on. It made him realise that nothing in life is easy. It gave him a respect for hard work, for perseverance, and for struggling to make your dream come through. It might not have been Lewis's dream to spend most of his life on a fishing boat, working in rough conditions, but he was still happy and proud to be looking after his family, and that attitude rubbed off on his son. The same applied to Grandpa Mitch. He too had a strong work ethic: indeed, he'd made his way from the old country with a tide of Italian immigrants determined to make a better life for themselves. He was no respecter of idleness, of shirking: he had worked hard throughout his whole life and he was to expect his grandson to do the same. It's just that when his grandson started work, it wasn't in a career any of the immediate family had enjoyed. It was to take them all by surprise.

Michael certainly wasn't offered an easy ride: he had to slog for many years before his talent was recognised and established and there were many times when he was tempted to give it all up. But, approaching his late teens, he and everyone else had begun to realise that his voice really was exceptional, and it might be the means by which he'd escape a life of hardship. And so his next move was one that has been tried and trusted. He began to enter local talent shows. But there were setbacks to be had there, too – until a chance meeting was to change his life.

2

A Long and Winding Road

Michael Bublé was sixteen years old, with a stark choice ahead of him. Having left school, he was in essence confronted with two options: to follow his father into the hard, precarious life of a fisherman, or to try to carve a career in the even more precarious world of show business. Both betokened a difficult way ahead; neither was an easy route. And so, for a while, he did both. Michael started singing in local clubs and bars, egged on and helped by Mitch, and then, in the summer, would go out with his father to work on the boats. And it was as well that he had that fallback, because his was an apprenticeship that was to last for years.

Michael spent several months a year for six years on the boat with his father, and there must have been times when he despaired of ever making a life for himself on shore. He was to look back on those months in the boat as a time of character building, a time when he learned to become a man, but back then it was hard. It was not what he wanted to do. Michael wanted to entertain. But how? How to get the influential people in the music industry to take any notice of him? Michael had no connections whatsoever within show business: a small-town boy from a working-class family of Italian immigrants, how was he going to get anyone to pay attention to him? (Then again, of course, one Francis Albert Sinatra came from similarly unpromising beginnings in Hoboken, New Jersey. But Michael, who was to be compared to Sinatra so often in the future, wasn't thinking about that back then.)

They say that what doesn't break you makes you stronger, and Michael was about to find out the truth of that. His route to the top was gruelling, and there were many times when he was tempted to give up altogether. But Michael's apprenticeship was helping to define his personal style. Playing in local clubs, performing wherever he could get a gig – and it was hard to get people to book him when he was starting out – gave him a chance to evolve his style away from the limelight. By the time people started noticing him, years later, he had finally refined his technique.

'I think it took me a while to find my voice,' he said in later years. 'When I started singing in clubs at sixteen, I was just stealing – just mimicking. I was taking what I liked about Harry Connick or Tony Bennett or Sinatra, or even taking what I liked about Otis Redding or Glen Campbell.' But he was learning as he did so, learning what suited him and what he could do. And for all the accusations of taking other people's styles, Michael now has a way of singing and moving that is undeniably his own. This was not developed after he finally got a good record deal: it came about through slogging his way through Vancouver's bars and nightclubs. It was a very hard lesson in honing his act, but one which Michael learned very well.

Grandpa was doing what he could. For a start, he paid for Michael to have singing lessons, which were paying off: at the age of sixteen, Michael entered a local talent contest and won. To this day, that remains the only formal training Michael has ever had. And then Mitch did what was to become the stuff of Bublé legend: he started offering free plumbing to local bandleaders if they would allow Michael to have a go. 'Isn't that hilarious?' said Michael. 'He'd put in, like, a hot-water dispenser or something so they would let me get up and sing.' It might have been hilarious, but it was true: 'Every Thursday we'd go out to the Ramada Inn,' Michael recalled. 'He'd bring me in and I'd sit in with some of the guys there.' This was a time Michael referred to frequently once he'd made it big. He has a robust sense of humour and the idea of Grandpa installing new loos so that his beloved Sunshine could have a go in the spotlight was one that continues to entertain.

At this stage, Michael was not earning a great deal, to put it mildly, and so he continued to go out in the summer with his father on the boat. This just made his ambition to be a singer all the stronger, because he was confronted with the alternative on a regular basis. 'You could make twenty thousand dollars a summer, but it was hard work, dangerous and physically demanding,' he said.

This was brought home by an incident that affected him profoundly. One night, in the early hours of the morning, his father woke him up to join in a search for a fisherman whose boat had overturned on the way home. Michael never forgot that. 'It really affected me,' he said. 'I couldn't stop thinking about his wife and kids. [Singing] even if I only made fifty dollars, by God, I didn't smell like fish, my hands weren't bleeding, I wasn't being woken at three thirty a.m. and working till midnight, so it was pretty cool for me.'

In fact, his whole time on the boat was to have a profound effect on him, and not just because it made him realise in later life how lucky he was. Michael has always been extremely proud of his Italian heritage, and there was something of the Latin male about the way he summed up his experiences on the boat and what they meant to him. 'The most deadly physical work I'll ever know in my lifetime,' he said. 'We'd be gone for two, sometimes three months at a time and the experience of living and working among guys over twice my age taught me a lot about responsibility and what it means to be a man.' This was a very different creature from the nerdy little boy at school, obsessed with the songs of swing: it marked the time that he really began to mature. Michael might not have made the grade as a professional singer yet, but he was proving that he had what it took to hold his own out there on the high seas.

He learned other lessons at that time, too. Because he had not been a jock at school, Michael still felt somewhat of an outsider; now, the fact that he was working for his father, who was in charge of all the men, slightly went to his head. For the first time, he was right at the centre of the action and went through a phase that foreshadowed the short period of big-headedness that he also went through when he finally achieved success. To his very great credit, when he started getting used to the fact that he was now a stratospherically successful singer, he acknowledged on a number of occasions both this early display of thoughtlessness and various periods of idiocy that still lay ahead.

'Four a.m. to eleven, four a.m. to eleven, every day,' he said, looking back to the earliest days in which he had worked on the boat. 'There was great camaraderie, but it was tough physically. And by sixteen, I had worked my way up to something like first mate. One year, we had this guy named Justin. He was twenty-six. Big. Six-five. And one day I told him, "Hey, chop the ice. Now. When I say jump, you say: 'How high?'" It led to a confrontation. He headbutted me, and said, "I don't care whose son you are. Don't take away my dignity."'

'Now I should have known that. My father never spoke to people that way. But it taught me common respect. And I never, ever, talk down to people.' Well – up to a point. In the years to come, when all the years of struggle had finally come to an end, Michael was to go through a pretty brattish phase when he certainly didn't display the manners his parents had taught him. But once he had got over that initial stage of bad behaviour, he learned his lesson and piped down. That was something else that came from his time on the boat.

Even when he was out on the boats, however, Michael seized every opportunity to sing that came his way, although his parents were not yet aware that he was losing no opportunity to pursue the path he wanted most. Lewis reminisced about it years later, when his son had finally made the grade. 'I remember when I used to have my Seine boat, the *Dalmacia*, and my son and crew would jump on a bus and go into Prince Rupert to have a few cold drinks,' he said. 'But, of course, they never told me anything until we left port – so later I heard Michael went to the Surf Club for karaoke night. There he was singing Elvis songs to a very tough-looking crowd. The rest of the crew was fearful for their lives. It turns out Michael was a real hit and the crowd ended up buying him drinks.' Again, it was all character building. These audiences might have been non-paying and involuntary, but they were still audiences and Michael was learning how to handle them. It is said that if a comic appeared on stage at the

Glasgow Apollo and the audience liked him, they would let him live. A similar philosophy could be applied here.

The Bublés, as has already been stated, were a fairly stolid working-class family, but a slight oddity had become apparent. Michael was not the only member of the family trying to make it in show business, and right at the start, he was actually being outshone. As he divided his time between working on the boats and trying to make it as a singer, his little sister Crystal had become an actress, and like her older brother's stage career, it was something that had been going on for some time. She, too, had started out as a teenager, and was now trying to make the grade.

When she was young, Crystal had been a fanatical dancer, as much so as her brother was a singer. She studied jazz, tap and ballet with Darcelle's Dancers, and would go out on to the teen dance circuit to compete. This came to an abrupt end when she was fifteen and hurt her ankle, at which point the very non-showbiz mother Amber stepped in to reassure her distraught offspring. It must have seemed as if everything was over, especially at that highly over-emotional age, but Amber was adamant that it was not so. 'My mom said, "Everything happens for a reason. Don't worry,"' she later recalled. 'I was like, "No." Then I started doing extra work on films, just to keep my mind busy. I was going crazy.' And, while not in a big way, it took off.

Crystal began to carve something of a show-business career of her own, appearing in films and television. Her first documented appearance was way back in 1996, when she appeared as Clover in *Madison*, before going on to other shows such as *Kissed* (admittedly as an extra), *Poltergeist: The Legacy*, *Breaker High*, *Christina's House* and various others. She wasn't mega famous and she didn't make a fortune, but she got by.

It was a strange coincidence that two children from such a resolutely non-showbiz background should choose to make that profession their own. Crystal acknowledged as much. 'I don't know what happened back there,' she said years later, after Michael became world famous. 'They've always been so open to whatever we wanted to do. It was nice, growing up, knowing that I was never forced into doing anything. Whether it was dancing or acting, I wasn't doing it for them. I was doing it for me.'

Michael felt the same. Not that the eldest child of the family seemed to be getting anywhere. Back in the early days it was pretty dispiriting. He was known as a great local talent, but Michael was aiming at the big time, not to become a big fish in a small pond. And it was now that his determination really came to the fore. 'He stuck to it and said, "If I can't do that, I won't do anything,"' Amber recalls. 'He just knew it. He told us when he was a kid, he was destined for it. I think he gets it from my sticking to it, I mean.' And stick to it he did. Michael was to get very depressed, right up to the point of almost giving up just before he finally made his break, but back in the early days, he was resolute. He was determined he was going to succeed.

Amber and Lewis were worried, however. Show business is one of the most difficult areas in which to make a success, and even if Michael did manage to get anywhere, the type of music he sang had, they believed, only a limited appeal. It was not as if their son wanted to become a rock star: Michael wanted to follow in the footsteps of the likes of Tony Bennett, and Bennett did not, at that stage at least, appeal to most of Michael's contemporaries. Who, other than people of Michael's parents' generation, listened to the Frank Sinatras of this world? The Tony Bennetts? The Dean Martins? Not only was Michael trying to make it in the hardest business of all, but he seemed almost wilfully to be picking an area in which he couldn't possibly succeed.

Michael recalled this much later on: 'All the people, including the people who love me, said that it's not going to happen. They said never expect that to happen for you because it won't. Because of the kind of music you make it'll have limited success, limited radio and all that.' But still he persevered.

It seemed like everyone was telling Michael his dreams couldn't come true. There was, however, one notable exception and that was Grandpa Mitch. Quite apart from anything else, he had an emotional investment himself in Michael's success, having done so much to encourage his grandson to choose this particular path, and he remained adamant that Michael would get there in the end. The encouragement continued. The singing lessons continued. The urging to learn even more of the old songs continued. He never gave up on what had become a dream for both of them.

'He was one of the people who never stopped believing in me,' Michael said, many years later. 'Even maybe when I stopped believing in myself, he was absolute that my career was going to happen the way it has. His friends used to argue with him and tell him he was crazy and that I was never going to amount to anything and that this music was dead.' The fact that even Mitch's friends were prepared to risk the wrath of their old mate by telling him his grandson had chosen the wrong path was significant. It is impossible to overstate quite how bleak the future seemed to be for Michael back then.

But he persevered. Acting appealed to Michael as well as singing and, aged seventeen, he was to get the part of Elvis, which he toured with in a production of *Red Rock Diner*. It garnered good reviews – 'Elvis lookalike Michael Bublé, Biker/Greaser/Heartthrob Curtis Blayne and blonde bomb-shell Lalainia Lindbjerg were all innovative, exciting, highly energetic and above all extremely talented in their roles,' wrote Wayne MacEachern of a performance at the Arts Club Theatre, Granville Island, a theatre that will be totally unfa-miliar to the readers of this book, because Broadway it wasn't. Not by a long shot. He also appeared in the musical *Forever Swing*, touring around north America with it. But still fame totally eluded him.

But in hindsight, he had happier memories, too. 'Yes, I can remember singing at the Georgia Bar and Grill, and when they hired me for [the Vancouver nightclub] Babalu, I was so excited,' he later recalled to one Vancouver journalist. Indeed, he was to become quite a fixture at Babalu, performing there regularly for at least two years. He retained a great affection for his home town. 'Bill Millerd of the Arts Club Theatre was invited to come down and see my act, and he was just starting the musical *Red Rock Diner*. I urged him to let me perform in the musical. He really felt I wasn't right for the show. He did come down, not once but four times, because he wasn't sure. I'm glad I was able to change his mind.'

Once more, it was invaluable experience. But once more, it failed to lead to anything else (although Michael did meet his first serious girlfriend, actress and dancer Debbie Timuss, who was to play a major part in his life during the ensuing years). That early determination was showing through, though: the fact that Michael was prepared to badger until he got the role was an early foreshadowing of the way he badgered David Foster, who was finally to make him a star, until Foster finally took him on. Still the major breakthrough failed to appear, however, and so with that first win in a local talent show behind him, aged eighteen, Michael decided to enter a second, in which he sang 'All Of Me'.

Again, he won and again it looked as if a major future awaited him. There was, however, a problem of such magnitude that Michael must have wondered if he was ever going to get an even break. After the show, he was approached by the organiser, Beverly Delich, who had established Silver Lining Management in 1989. A tough cookie who had brought on a lot of the local talent, she certainly saw something in Michael, even if she wasn't entirely sure what it was. But the problem remained. 'How old are you?' she asked.

'Eighteen,' Michael replied.

'I have some good news and some bad news,' she said. 'You won. But you're disqualified. Underage.'

Michael retold this story much later on in his own inimitable way. 'I entered a talent contest at the Big Bamboo club in Vancouver,' he recalled. 'I was only sixteen and the law said you had to be nineteen to get into a club. I drew on a moustache and sideburns, snuck in and won the contest. The next day when I spoke to Beverly Delich, who ran the place, she told me I was underage and had been disqualified. Despite that she became my manager and we spent ten wonderful years working together.' Michael was not being entirely serious, of course, especially about that moustache, and he compressed various events together in order to make his point. Michael did take part in two talent shows in the early days, not just the one, and his success must have shown him that at least some members of the public rated him. It was not just his family that thought he one day deserved to be a star.

But still. Michael was, after all, eighteen: to be underage at that stage was a heavy blow indeed. But all was not lost. It was becoming apparent that this dark cloud did have a silver lining. Bev might not have been able to give Michael his award, but she realised that a serious talent had turned up on the stage. And so she encouraged Michael to enter the Canadian Youth Talent Search, which turned out to prove to him, at least, that he was on the right track. He was the 1995 winner: this was the boost he finally needed, and it helped him finally to persuade Bev to become his manager. Michael badgered her to do so, as he had badgered in the past and would badger again, even promising her fifteen per cent of all his earnings.

'Michael. What's fifteen per cent of nothing?' she replied. Eventually, however, she agreed to sign on.

Although the chances are that Michael would have made it whatever manager he chose, Bev was an inspired choice. Once she'd decided to link her fate with his, she was determined her young protégé was going to make the grade, and so began an onslaught to help him make it big. Not that anyone else seemed to appreciate this just yet: Bev found she was getting no further with Michael than Michael himself had found before he managed to persuade her to take him on. 'Some mornings I'd cry at the breakfast table, but I knew he had it,' she recalled. Not many other people were so sure, though, including, at times, Michael himself. He was feeling increasingly disillusioned and unsure whether he'd made the right decision by pursuing a career in show business. Just what was it going to take before he finally made the grade?

Well, his manager, for a start. Bev was, in many ways, the making of Michael. Grandpa Mitch had introduced him to the music, paid for his singing lessons, cajoled and wheedled his friends into allowing Michael to perform and, more importantly than anything else, given him the emotional support he needed when it looked as if he was never going to get anywhere, but he didn't actually know the music business.

Bev did. She was able to provide him with his first proper guidance, and give him some much needed credibility within the business, as well as, like Grandpa, offering him encouragement and support. It was to stand her in good stead, too, as a judge of who really had what it took to make it in the most fickle and volatile industry in the world, and as a person who had the guts to back her hunch. The Silver Lining Management website still boasts of her involvement with the very young Michael, although it is years since she gave up managing him on a day-to-day basis: her judgement, even though it took a while to prove it, was to turn out to be spectacularly correct.

Other people realised this, too. The jazz musician and composer Gabriel Mark Hasselbach, who became a friend of Michael's, is convinced that Bev was a fundamental reason for his success. 'Bev was Michael's ticket out of Burnaby,' he said. 'She took that boy by the collar and dragged him to fame.' Success, however, did not come overnight. Michael put his all into it, but his all was not enough: he played every venue that would have him – bars, clubs, shopping malls and one memorable stint as a Santa Claus. He got paid $80 for that.

Small acting roles followed, so small that he wasn't even credited with being on screen. For a start, he managed to find a tiny role in the television series *Death Game*, about a group of survivors after an earthquake in Los Angeles, a drama so cheesy it wouldn't be the highlight of anyone's CV, let alone someone who appeared in the role of 'Drome Groupie'. He also appeared in *The X Files* a couple of times in 1996, in the episodes 'Apocrypha' and 'Piper Maru', both times as a submarine sailor and both times uncredited. It was no way to make a living and was extremely discouraging. Michael's first national television appearance was in an award-winning Bravo! documentary called *Big Band Boom*, directed by Mark Glover Masterson. Did it do anything for his career? No.

But it was the music that mattered most and despite everything, Michael never held himself back once he was up on stage. He might have been increasingly disillusioned by day, but by night, once up on that stage, he showed himself to be the charismatic performer he really was. This might not yet have been the big time, but Michael behaved as if it was. He had an audience, and even if it wasn't yet the audience he actually wanted, Michael was determined to put on a good show.

Someone who was to become his friend, Buzz Bishop, a DJ in Vancouver, recalled that Michael always put heart and soul into his performance, quite as much as he would have done were he on a major stage instead of a local club. 'Michael would put all his energy and passion into it,' he said. 'He treated every show as if he were headlining in Vegas.' At that stage, Vegas seemed a possibility so remote that it was barely worth thinking about. But still Michael dreamed, and sang, and hoped for a brilliant future.

He was certainly gaining a degree of sophistication: Michael the small-town boy, son of a fisherman, was beginning his metamorphosis into global crooner. But it was massively dispiriting at times. Michael might have been giving it his all, but the audience certainly wasn't: he was, quite literally, the background music to the fun they were about to have. He knew it, too. 'They came to meet a woman or get wasted, but I learned my craft,' he said. 'It taught me how not to reek of desperation, how to step back and try to be charismatic and let them fall in love with me.'

At around this time, Michael was to record the first of three records he made independently, one of which was to be absolutely invaluable to his later success. The very first of these was titled, appropriately enough, *First Dance*, and he recorded it towards the end of 1995. The cover shows the young Michael sporting a quiff and bearing a distinct resemblance to the young Elvis. The six tracks were 'Learnin' the Blues', 'I've Got You Under My Skin', 'Just One More Dance', 'All of Me', 'One Step At a Time' and 'I'll Be Seeing You'.

It made no impact whatsoever on the world at the time, but this, and the other two independent albums Michael brought out before he hit the big time, are now collectors' items. Whole internet chains have been established trying to track them down (for a Bublé fan, finding one of these records is equivalent to stumbling across a signed first edition of an early J. K. Rowling). *Babalu* (2001) and *Dream* (2002) were to follow. At the time, though, it was the equivalent of vanity publishing, a present to Grandpa, who had stood by him for ever, and who continued to keep the faith. No one realised this was the foreshadowing of a great career. Who was Michael Bublé? Still just a small-town kid.

At around this time, Michael and his now live-in girlfriend, Debbie Timuss, moved to Toronto, where they hoped they'd get more opportunities – though, in many ways, they didn't. 'I thought a bigger city might finally bring me a break,' Michael explained. But the work remained sporadic and it didn't make him happy: 'Mostly I was playing the sort of places where people went to get drunk or to get laid,' said Michael, in an echo of what he'd said about his gigs in

Vancouver. 'They certainly didn't come to hear me.' He was frequently discouraged and just about always broke.

And even when Michael did get paid well, which didn't happen very often, his overheads were such that he made no money at all. 'I'd be paid a thousand dollars a night, but I'd hire six of the best musicians and pay them a hundred and fifty each, and I'd walk away with the cab fare home,' Michael recalled. 'The crummy thing was I was making such poor money, and I was starting to go into debt. My musicians were getting more than I was.'

Bev and Mitch hadn't given up, but Michael himself was seriously considering doing so. He hadn't expected to make it overnight, but it had been years now, and nothing – not Bev's work on his behalf, nor the move to Toronto – had put him anywhere near the spotlight in which he wanted to bask. Michael was not overtly vain, but he needed some comeback, some recognition that he was a talented singer who had a great deal to offer, and he wasn't getting that at all.

There was the future to think of, too. Michael was still a young man, still in his very early twenties, but he had to be practical and think of where all this was going. One thing he emphatically did not want to do was pursue a career that was never going to lead anywhere, and he became so despondent, he seriously began to contemplate giving it all up. 'But, yeah, at some point I thought to myself, "Oh God, I want to be a dad at some point, and I can't keep living on potential,"' Michael told one interviewer.

That point about children cropped up again in another interview. 'I was about to give up, not because I felt sorry for myself, but because at some point I wanted to be a husband and a father,' said Michael. 'I knew that if I continued on, the harder it is to get back into real life. It's not that I wasn't talented, I just didn't get that break . . . if I was serious about wanting to have a life and make money, I knew that I would have to probably go back to school. I was thinking of going into the media, maybe as a television reporter or something like that. I enjoy my relationship with the camera. I have no problem being in front of the cameras.' He had, after all, had experience of that in his tiny television roles.

He was being quite serious, too: Michael was getting so despondent that he really was thinking of giving it all up. But his family, especially Grandpa Mitch, refused to lose faith in him, while Bev Delich was horrified at the very thought. 'I told him, "Michael, go ahead,"' she said. 'And in a few years, when you see some other singer creeping up, making it big with the same songs you sing, you'll regret it for the rest of your life. And wish you could slash your wrists.' It was a far-sighted strategy on her part. Michael kept at it, difficult as he found it at times.

Michael also voiced doubts about the future to Gabriel Hasselbach, saying that he was considering giving it all up. Hasselbach was not impressed. 'How ludicrous that sounded to a veteran like me,' he said. 'It takes years of dues-paying to expect a payoff. Michael, in his early twenties, expected it tomorrow. It just goes to show you the power of intention. He drew fame to himself like a magnet.'

Indeed, at other times, always encouraged by the faithful Bev, Michael was as determined as he ever had been. 'I've never met anyone so hungry for success,' said Kerry Gold, a journalist based in Vancouver. 'His manager Beverly would hound me to come see him perform. The young girls were transfixed. It's hard not to like Michael, because he has this way of making you feel like you're part of his inner circle, even when you're in the media. I think that's part of the reason for his success. He charms people.' That was to come back to haunt Michael very unexpectedly indeed, once he'd finally made it and made the mistake of treating a journalist as a friend – but that was all yet to come.

3

The Wedding Singer

Michael had had enough. It was 2000, the new millennium, and he had been on the road for years. Where had he got? Nowhere. For all the effort he'd made, all the feelers he'd put out, the performances, the independently produced records and the unstinting support of his family, he'd drawn a big, fat zero. There are few fields in which it is harder to shine than entertainment and Michael was beginning to feel that that was it. He was just another soon to be has-been, a nearly made it who never quite got that lucky break. Was it worth it? No.

Well, yes, actually, because after all these years, Michael was finally about to get the break he'd been looking for. It was not before time. He was as close as he'd ever come to quitting the music business. He considered retraining as an electrician, and there was always the option of his father's boat. But deep down, Michael was still desperate to make it in show business. He was as near as he ever had been to feeling despair. Music was an integral part of his life and it was beginning to feel that he was going to fail in the area he'd set his heart on. It was a heavy burden for a young man to bear.

Michael's attitude could be summed up years later by a very downbeat description he gave of his life at that time. 'I had moved to Toronto with my girlfriend, trying to make it, figuring it's a bigger city,' he said, sounding slightly like the boxer in the Simon and Garfunkel song of the same name. 'My girlfriend was doing musical theatre, and she was bringing home the bacon and paying for rent and all that other stuff. At some point, a big tour gig ended, and we had no money. I couldn't afford to go home. So I took a corporate, a really kind of shoddy corporate gig for a couple, whatever it was, three thousand bucks or something, and it was enough to get me home.'

But it didn't have to. It was at this bleak stage in his career that Michael was to be offered the gig that was going to change his life. Not that it was immediately apparent: at first it seemed like just another corporate function, of the type he'd done so many times before, and was clearly beginning to loathe. But this time, someone was sitting in the audience who was to prove the catalyst for one of the most glittering careers in recent show business history: Michael McSweeney, who was a friend, associate and sometime speechwriter of the former Canadian Prime Minister Brian Mulroney. Breaking off from the chatter around him, the older man began to listen more carefully to what was going on up on stage and liked what he heard. Michael wasn't just some run-of-the-mill entertainer: this was a guy with an extraordinary voice, glittering talent, and a huge charisma on stage. Somehow, McSweeney knew he was looking at a star. At the end of the evening, he made himself known to his young namesake, who in turn gave him one of the self-produced albums to take away with him. It was to prove a fortuitous gift, not that Michael Bublé realised it at the time. 'If you and your wife like it, great,' he said. 'If you don't, it'll make a great coaster.' It was to do a good deal more than that.

McSweeney's friendship with Brian Mulroney was going to prove a turning point for Michael Bublé, for he thought Mulroney and his wife Mila might like the CD, and passed the album on to them. The couple just happened to be planning the wedding of their daughter, Caroline, to the son of *Harper's* magazine editor Lewis Lapham. Preparations were already far advanced, and so bringing someone new into the proceedings did not immediately seem to be an option. But after she'd listened to it, Mila liked the album so much, she had a great idea. Why not ask the artist to come and sing on the night? Michael was a local boy, which was all to the good, but more than that, he had a voice to send tingles up your spine. Who better to serenade the happy couple and their guests?

Brian Mulroney wasn't so sure. 'My first reaction was to say to Mila, look, you've already put together a magnificent wedding, with bands galore,' he recalled. 'Our friend David Foster was going to perform, and Kathie Lee Gifford was going to sing. And she said, "But take a listen to this CD." When I did, I couldn't believe it. I said right away, "This guy's a cross between Bobby Darin and Frank Sinatra."' It was exactly the response Michael needed – and, from all people, the ex-Canadian Prime Minister. Would it have been possible to meet anyone more influential than that? Events began to gather pace, and fast.

If Michael had a guardian angel who had arranged events to benefit him, the guardian angel couldn't have done better than what came next. One of the men present at the wedding reception was the above-mentioned David Foster. He was very well known as a Grammy award-winning record producer, and an executive with Warner Brothers, with a spectacular track record behind him, having worked with, among others, Madonna, Celine Dion, Cher, Barbra Streisand, Lionel Richie, Josh Groban and Whitney Houston. If ever there was a fortuitous occasion to have a particular person sitting in your audience, this was it. And as Michael took to the stage, and belted his heart out, Foster immediately realised he was watching a potential star. 'Brian was beside me, beaming, "Wait'll you hear this kid, wait'll you hear this kid,"' he recalled. 'I was going, "Come on, man, I just want to enjoy the wedding."' But then Michael came on and, according to Foster, he 'hit the stage like a lightning bolt'. All those years doing the clubs; all those venues when Michael gave it to them like they were in Las Vegas, not some downtown dive in Vancouver, were coming to fruition. He needed to prove himself that night – and he did.

Michael himself was well aware what was going on. The Mulroneys had really taken up his cause: he had become their project, their protégé, and they wanted to give him all the help they could. And they were in a position to do so, too. 'Mila loved that style of music and they wanted me to have a chance to showcase for him [David Foster],' Michael said. 'They were very generous. It was the biggest moment of my life, I can tell you. The Mulroneys had me over for dinner in Montreal. They were just unbelievably sweet to me. They said, "You're wonderful, you're great – David Foster needs to work with you because you deserve your shot."' And so there was that weight of expectation, too – Michael knew the Mulroneys were doing everything they could to help him. It wasn't just for himself that he was singing. He simply couldn't let them down.

The next day, Foster had the chance to listen to the young marvel again: the Mulroneys were hosting a lunch party, during which Michael sang some solo numbers, including Kurt Weill's 'Mack the Knife': at one point, Mulroney himself joined Michael on stage. Michael had potential: Mulroney did not. But still, there were worries, for in the music business nothing ever runs smoothly: 'Yeah, I really heard it,' David Foster later recalled of that lunch. 'I heard the vision. But also we have to look at music business slots. Is there a slot open? And that slot, the young crooner, was available. Harry Connick Jr had opened the door wide, then walked away from it to do movies and other things.' And so Michael Bublé walked through that door. The time was right, the person was right. But there was still going to be quite a mountain to climb.

Michael was ready to do so, too. Having come perilously close to quitting the music scene altogether, and now being presented with a big break like this, he was going to do everything in his power to make it work. As he recalled it later, it was an amazing opportunity, one which he made the most of, not least because he'd waited for so long and knew an opening like this might never come along again. He had wanted this for so long and now, finally, it was within his grasp.

'Of course, I jumped at the chance,' he said. 'Actually, at that time I was doing a lot of my originals. So that's what I sang. I got up on stage and did a bunch of my originals and Foster, I guess, was taken with it. He came up to me and said, "You're pretty good, kid. Do you want to come down to LA next week?" And I thought, "Oh my God, I've made it."'

Foster was a very canny choice on the part of the Mulroneys for another reason, too. Not only did he have some of the aristocracy of showbiz on his books, but he was also responsible for the success of Josh Groban. Like Michael,

Josh was not necessarily an obvious mainstream choice: he did not have a career that could be pushed through radio airplay, as his music would not fit naturally into many radio playlists. It was thought, back then, that Groban's music wouldn't appeal to a mass audience because it was jazz rather than mainstream rock, and the jazz boom that was about to take off was still in its early stages. But Foster had made his career a roaring success and so was open to the idea of finding another young entertainer who he could push to similarly stratospheric heights. In Michael, he had found that man. But he was not yet ready to commit to it. A few more hoops had to be jumped through first.

Rather crucially, although he was now mixing in circles a lifetime away from those in which he was brought up, Michael was not unnerved by it all. Had he been too awestruck at that stage of the game, it could easily have gone badly wrong: as it was, he held his own. 'I'm not nervous around people of affluence,' he said. 'I enjoyed meeting them [the ex-PM and the record producer]. They are really nice guys.' He flew to Malibu the next week. Mulroney, David Foster – he could cope with hanging out with these people. It sure beat the hell out of some Vancouver dive.

But it would be jumping the gun to say that Michael's career path now took off smoothly, without a glance back. For although Foster was the right man to guide Michael's career, and despite the fact that he had already made a success of Josh Groban, he had not reached such a prominent position in the music business by making expensive mistakes, and he was determined to make sure that Michael really was going to be the next big thing before he committed himself. He had the voice, all right, and the on-stage charisma, but would that translate into music sales? No one could be sure.

It was now up to Michael to convince Foster, once and for all, that he, Michael, was worth taking a bet on. And so, for a start, Michael relocated to Los Angeles: that's where Foster was, where the action was, where the money was, and where, for a time, Michael needed to be. Next, he set about proving his worth. Desperate for Foster to agree to produce him, Michael continued to badger him: finally, Foster said that if Michael was able to raise the $500,000 cost of producing the first album, he, Foster, would take him on. Michael did exactly that: he went out and found investors – including Paul Anka, who himself had started as a Canadian crooner – who thought he had a future in front of him and were prepared to put their money where their mouths were. In the end, Foster's record label, 143 Records, covered the (significantly higher) costs.

Everyone else involved was a lot older than Michael and it's hard to escape the conclusion that they were all thoroughly enjoying helping the young man on his way. 'When I first heard Michael, not one label would touch him,' Anka recalled some years later, in an interview about his own work. 'With arranger David Foster, together we spent a couple of months working with him, picking music that suited his vocal style. With someone as talented as Michael, all you can do is guide them to where they want to go. It was so exciting to be a part of that experience, I wanted to do the same for myself and find new material that suited me.' Anka and Foster had both been so successful for so long that they'd almost forgotten what it was like to be young and struggling, and there was something thrilling about being reminded so forcefully of their own pasts. And they were all Canadian, too. That certainly wasn't the reason Foster and Anka ultimately put their heads above the parapet for Michael, but it gave an added frisson to the mix.

It was what Michael had spent years waiting for. But it wasn't all music at that stage of his life. It was during this early period of his breakthrough, when Michael was first based in Los Angeles, that he started to do some film work. It was all grist to the mill, provided him with some much needed income and, indeed, added to the buzz that was slowly growing about him. There had been that early acting work on television, but now he was appearing in the big league – albeit sometimes in little more than walk-on roles – with some of the huge Hollywood stars. Michael appeared as a karaoke singer opposite Gwyneth Paltrow and Huey Lewis in *Duets* in 2000: he belted out 'Strangers in the Night' on screen. 'I play Michael Bublé and that's very tough,' said Michael melodramatically to one interviewer. 'He's a very complex person.' This was followed by a belly laugh.

Next up was an acting role, as Van Martin, a club owner, in *Totally Blonde*. And another role followed, as Hap in the film *The Snow Walker*, which was released in the year Michael's proper debut album came out, 2003. That year also saw him in an episode of *Days of Our Lives* – but his singing career was soon to take precedence over anything else.

Finally, Michael's persistence paid off: he convinced Foster – not, in truth, that he needed much convincing – of his worth. Foster then got his new protégé signed up with 143 Records, which was part of Warner Bros, but which received no assurance of support at that stage from its powerful parent company. This really was taking a shot in the dark. Indeed, such were the mutterings that it was even suggested to Michael that he change his name to Santaga, Grandpa Mitch's surname, as it sounded slightly like Sinatra. Much as he adored his grandfather, Michael knew that such a move would be exceedingly distressing to his father, and refused. That took some guts – he had not, by this stage, actually shown that he could cut the mustard and was still dependent on his new record company for everything. Above all, he needed David Foster. And so together, the duo began work on his first internationally acclaimed CD.

143 Records had quite a history. Originally it was started by David Foster in the 1990s – the numbers refer to the number of letters in three words, I Love You. But its parent label was Reprise, founded by Frank Sinatra, the man with whom Michael was to be so often compared. Nor was Sinatra the only big name associated with the label: other performers included Joni Mitchell, Jimi Hendrix, The Corrs and Neil Young. Michael was clearly happy in his new home. 'It's a very eclectic record company, too,' he said later, harking back to those years. 'We have some acts that no one gave a chance but all of a sudden we sell millions of records – Josh Groban, Enya, me – now we're all proving them wrong.'

He enjoyed the work, too. Michael had, of course, made records before, but nothing on this scale. This was the big time, and he knew it. He'd swapped the Vancouver dives for hour upon hour upon hour at the recording studio, but this was what he'd been aiming at. And he loved every minute of it. He was working closely with people who were not only the biggest names in the business, but who had faith in him and who were encouraging him. What young singer wouldn't have been beside himself with happiness in such a place? 'It was a blast,' Michael recalled. 'Seven months of hard work every day but really, really rewarding. We did some of it at Sony but most of it at Chartmaker. When we had to use strings and stuff we would go to Paramount. Most of the vocals we did at Chartmaker, which is David's home studio.'

Other big names were now coming on board, too. David Foster had taken a massive personal risk on signing Michael up: for all the success of people like Groban, Michael still did not fit into the mainstream and there was no assurance about how his career would go. And so Foster turned to old associates and friends for advice, for back-up and for support. In doing so, he proved that he was not alone in his faith in his new signing, while at the same time, the involvement of other powerful figures in the music industry continued to contribute that all-important buzz.

The second part of the Canadian triumvirate, Paul Anka, of course, was asked increasingly for his input, which he happily gave. Michael and Paul hit it off immediately. 'Paul Anka was executive producer and he came and supervised sometimes and always gave us good tips and pointers. He's a good guy,' said Michael with commendable understatement.

There then followed a consultation about who should be Michael's manager. Beverly Delich had provided staunch support, but while she was a highly successful woman in her home town, a future was now being envisaged for Michael on another scale altogether. And Beverly was not quite the right person to give him the guidance he now needed – not on her own, at least, for she did continue to work with Michael even when new people came in. Enter Bruce Allen, also from Vancouver, who managed a huge stable of stars, including Bryan Adams, Anne Murray and Martina McBride. He was the big league, the third part of the Canadian triumvirate, and if truth be told, Michael had been trying to attract his interest for years.

'I'm nearly sixty,' Allen recalled a few years later, 'and when I was growing up, the music was all about girlfriends, boyfriends. So I said, "Well, I've got to hear the record."

When I heard it, I realised it was really solid. He would bring romance to the music business.' But the story is also a credit to Beverly Delich, who realised that other hands were needed to boost her protégé. She'd done a huge amount to help Michael, but now other people were needed to give it that one last push. Michael now had the backing of three enormously powerful and influential men. The industry was really beginning to sit up and take note, although there were still some doubters: the head of Warner Bros was said to have announced that he'd be pleased if this unknown singer of fifty-year-old songs managed 100,000 in sales.

It was almost certain by that point that Michael would have made it whatever happened, given that he now had such powerful men rooting for him, but again he was the recipient of serious luck and goodwill in what happened next. Back in Canada, the Mulroneys were taking a keen interest in Michael's progress, and were delighted to see he was doing so well. But they didn't leave anything to chance. When he was in New York, Brian Mulroney had lunch with Bob Pittman, then the head of Time Warner, which owned Warner Bros, and lost no time in singing Michael's praises.

The Mulroneys also encouraged their Palm Beach neighbours, Paul and Jackie Desmarais, to have Michael sing in front of a crowd of very high-powered guests, as well as throwing his name in front of the likes of Merv Griffin, the renowned television entertainer who also owned a string of hotels, and Nancy Reagan. All of this was helping Michael to build a huge profile – and his debut album still wasn't out. 'I thought Michael was a tremendously talented young man, an outstanding Canadian,' Mulroney explained. 'But, I thought, there are all kinds of talented people around. I've also believed we all need a break in life.'

Michael was certainly getting his now. After months and months of blood, sweat and tears, his first album, *Michael Bublé*, was released on 11 February 2003. It contained standard classics including 'Fever', 'The Way You Look Tonight', 'For Once In My Life', 'Moondance', 'You'll Never Find Another Love Like Mine' and 'How Can You Mend a Broken Heart', with yet another member of the show business aristocracy, Barry Gibb of the Bee Gees, singing back-up vocals on that last song. Thanks entirely to Bruce Allen, it came out to the kind of media blitz more usually associated with stars who had been around as long as Bryan Adams. In the days following the release of the album, Michael was everywhere: in *People* magazine, on the *Today* show . . . everywhere. Album sales began gathering momentum: there was now about him more than ever the all-important buzz.

As interest in the new singer mounted, there was also some bemusement that Michael, an old style crooner after the fashion of Dean Martin, was doing so well. Most brand-new chart sensations were singing totally new material: here was Michael, singing the classics that had enchanted several generations even before he was born. Was this retro-chic, he was asked. Michael thought not. 'Honestly, I think whatever I do is organic,' he said, in the first of many, many interviews in which he was forced to defend what he did.

'I think I don't pretend to be something I'm not. I'm a young man. I realise we've had rap and rock 'n' roll. I don't pretend that never happened. I work very hard at being a consummate entertainer. I feel pretty at ease with an audience, I like to connect with them very much. I have great respect for this music. I like to think I have a good sense of personal style when it comes to this music. I don't want young people to think it's cheesy. Because it doesn't have to be cheesy.' It wasn't. A new audience was lapping it up. For every naysayer – and there were quite a few of them – who complained that Michael was singing the songs of a different era, there were fans stampeding out to buy the record. It was selling – massively so. And ultimately, that was all that counted.

Heavy promotional work continued. Michael travelled to many parts of the world: to Singapore, South Africa, the Philippines, the UK, Canada, South America and, of course, all over the United States. The album's performance in the last of these was, in fact, a disappointment: it only reached the top fifty of the *Billboard* 200, although three tracks, 'Kissing a Fool', 'How Can You Mend a Broken Heart' and 'Sway', all reached the top thirty of the *Billboard* Hot Adult Contemporary Tracks chart. But in the rest of the world it was a different story: the album made the top ten in the UK, Michael's homeland Canada, and South Africa, and reached number one in Australia. It also reached number thirty-three on the ARIA Top 100 Albums of 2003.

In other words, it was a great success. Michael himself, however, had slightly mixed feelings about the album. He didn't say so at the time: some years later, however, when he had become an established name, he voiced doubts over the final product – while acknowledging that there wasn't really any other way of doing it. 'David's balls were on the line,' he said. 'Two million dollars had been spent and he told me, "I can't afford to let you make this record. You'll have to trust me. I'm going to make it safe and marketable." And it worked. He introduced a nobody to the world.'

That intensive touring, often playing quite small venues – Michael was still a long way from being a household name – performed another function, too. The nature of the music meant that airplay was always going to be limited, which equally meant that it was essential that Michael actually got out there and showed what he could do. In addition to that, it was generally agreed that one of his great strengths was as a live performer, so it would hardly hurt him to strut his international stuff. And if more were needed, it would also convince Warner Bros that in Michael they had a young man who was prepared to put in the hours. He was working as hard as they were in the bid to establish himself as a star. And again, all those years getting nowhere were really paying off. Michael had learned how to handle an audience, how to play to their strengths, get them to respond to him. His voice, on the records, was magnificent. But out there, live on stage, he had them eating right out of his hand.

John Reid, at the time managing director of Warner Bros in London and subsequently executive vice-president for marketing for Warner Bros International, was clear they had a winner on their hands. 'We saw enormous success early on with Michael,' he said. 'His personality is infectious and he was an artist willing to travel at the drop of a hat. He would get off a plane in one country, work hard there, then get on another plane. It's wonderful to have an artist who is ready, willing and able to do that and a manager who supports that strategy.' It was hardly surprising, though. Michael had been around long enough to see the opposite: failure. He wasn't going to let a chance like this pass him by.

Still his guardian angel continued to watch over him. For all the hard work, you need a few lucky breaks, and Michael was continuing to get those. In Britain, it was an appearance on the Michael Parkinson show that really kicked his career off in the UK, and Michael didn't forget that. 'When Michael Parkinson hears a recording he likes, he'll invite the singer on to his show and that one appearance can transform a career,'

Michael recalled in 2005. 'He did it for Jamie Cullum, Il Divo and Clare Teal and last year he was my champion. If a career can rest on a single appearance like that, it says a lot about how jazz and easy listening music is constantly overlooked.'

As Michael's fame began to grow, he was increasingly asked about whom he modelled himself on. The answer was unsurprising, but it included some more recent singers, too. And it was a mark of how well Michael was doing that he was now spending time with some of the really big stars out there, who clearly saw him as the man to carry the flame of the music they so loved. 'I looked to Sinatra and Bennett and Bobby Darin and tried to borrow from them,' he recalled of that early period. 'I'm lucky enough to say I got to hang out with Tony Bennett a lot and even people like Engelbert Humperdinck, who has been really cool, and to ask them questions and get their support. That's been huge.'

Michael was keen to emphasise, however, that while the music he loved came from the past (or some of it did, at least), he was a modern man, very much of his own time. 'I wish I was more nostalgic about it, but I'm really not,' he said. 'I was born in 1975. I don't know what to do without a remote. I'm a young guy singing songs that are timeless, taking my experiences and wins and losses and the love my family gave me into my music. These songs are timeless. I listen to all these songs, everything from Oasis to Mel Tormé, Sinatra to Prince. I'm just taking songs I love and thinking, "How can I make this mine? Is there a way to reinvent this tune? It went to number one once, why can't it go twice?" Some of these songs should be celebrated. I'm an interpreter.'

He wasn't just an interpreter, though: he was a performer in his own right. And as Michael was increasingly recognised all around the world as an up and coming artist, so he began to be recognised in his personal life, too. Fans began approaching him for autographs, something that, even a few months previously, would have been unthinkable. They had also tracked down Michael's parents, with the result that Lewis and Amber had to change their telephone number. 'It's just going to get weirder,' Michael said at the time. And despite the lack of major US success, sales of the album, now in the hundreds of thousands, were beginning to exceed expectation. After nearly a decade on the road, Michael was on the verge of becoming a major star. (His father's career, incidentally, was also prospering – Lewis had been appointed a member of the British Columbia Salmon Marketing Council. The whole family was doing well.)

How fast did he become a star after this? Pretty fast. In an interview he gave fairly soon after his breakthrough, after some intensive touring of the world, Michael asserted that not many people actually recognised him on the street. Beverly Delich, delighted that her young discovery was turning into such a success, begged to differ, reminding him of an incident when they went to get his passport just before the tours began. 'We got to the wicket and the guy said, "Oh my God."' He photocopied Michael's driving licence and got the young Bublé to autograph the photocopy for his wife. This kind of thing was happening increasingly frequently.

He was also beginning to experience the joys of female attention. Michael was young, handsome, vibrant and charismatic (he also had a girlfriend), and girls were beginning to make it plain they found him very attractive. Michael did not have a problem with this. 'I love it, I love it!' he told one interviewer. 'Anyone who tells you they don't, they're lying. It's a great thing. How cool is my life! I was having my picture taken last night with three beautiful women, and I said to myself, "I love my job!"' The high school nerd was well and truly long gone.

Michael's happiness at his success was a very understandable reaction, especially having struggled so hard to get to where he was now. And Michael was too right: the vast majority of young men would love to find themselves at the centre of excessive female attraction, whatever they might have said to the contrary. But the temptation in such a situation is to let it get out of hand, as Michael himself was later to admit. Fame and money are a heady combination for anyone, especially a young man, and to go from relative obscurity to international heartthrob in a matter of months is difficult for someone who is just not used to that kind of attention. And so it was to prove.

But that was yet to come. At present, Michael was just lapping up the fact that he was in the spotlight, at last. His only complaint was that he didn't have enough time for ice hockey: 'The only thing I really don't like about this whole thing, is that I haven't really been able to have one hour to go and work out and I'm getting a little stir-crazy,' he said. 'I need to get my hockey stick in my hand and go for a little skate. But this is what I worked for for so long and what I dreamt of.' Miss hockey he might, but it was a small price to pay.

Of course, Grandpa Mitch was absolutely loving this, too. This massive success was his dream as well as Michael's, and as he saw his grandson attaining ever higher heights of fame, he could scarcely contain his pride. Michael rang him regularly to keep him in touch with what was going on and it was hard to know whether grandfather or grandson was the more taken aback by everything that was happening. As he featured on yet another prestigious TV slot, Michael confided to one interviewer, 'I called my grandpa and said, "*Dateline* is doing a story. Can you believe this? *Dateline*." And he said, "What took them so long?"'

Lewis and Amber, meanwhile, were watching the growing furore centred on their son open-mouthed. Young Michael, their boy, who had been out on the boats with his father until so recently, was now at the centre of all this? A journalist went to visit them on their boat and found Amber poring over publications featuring her increasingly famous son: 'Here he is in *People* – then there's this one, *Flare*, and last week's *TV Week* and this one is *New York Night Life*,' she said. 'He just finished a shoot for *Vanity Fair*, which should come out in August, I think.' Her pride in her boy was palpable.

Lewis was equally astounded. 'Every show is sold out,' he said. 'Nobody could have believed it would have taken off like it has. You wouldn't think children would like it. But you've got three generations going to his concerts. Nineteen-year-olds are going nuts and 89-year-olds are going nuts.' Indeed, this was to be key to Michael's success. He had enormous intergenerational appeal, with whole families buying into his music. He frequently used his stage performances to sympathise, jokingly, with the men in the audience who'd been dragged out by their wives and girlfriends, but if truth be told, he was building quite a following of male fans, too.

There was humour in the Bublés' new situation, too, as both parents acknowledged. Here were they, a blue-collar family from British Columbia, and suddenly their son was mixing with some of the biggest stars in the world. 'Kevin Spacey calls him all of the time, Dustin Hoffman – they both follow all of his shows,' Lewis said. As for Brian Mulroney – 'I'll pick up the phone and it will be Brian looking for Michael,' Lewis continued. 'I just shake my head.' Nor did it stop there: Lewis remembered when they all went to visit David Foster. 'His house looks like a Mexican resort,' he said. 'They have trams that take you up and down. And there's David Foster talking with Paul Anka about their jets and I'm thinking about using the Mr Lube coupon in my pocket.'

More acclaim followed. In November 2003, Michael released a Christmas EP, *Let It Snow*, with five new tracks. It, too, did well, although it only got to fifty-six on the *Billboard* 200: again, Australia showed itself to be a fan, with the title track reaching the top forty. The momentum was gathering. In 2004, Michael released a CD/DVD called *Come Fly With Me*: the CD had three new studio tracks, two live recordings of new songs and three live recordings of songs from the *Michael Bublé* album. Meanwhile, the DVD contained live footage and behind-the-scenes footage of the world tour. A couple of songs from the original CD, 'For Once In My Life' and 'Kissing a Fool', also featured in the 2003 film *Down With Love*, starring Renée Zellweger and Ewan McGregor, as did Michael's duet with Holly Palmer in a performance of the film's title song.

Michael appeared to be getting disillusioned with that aspect of his career, however. Asked if he wanted to pursue acting, he replied, 'I don't think so. It's too easy to spread yourself too thin. And soundtracks are a real crapshoot. You just don't know what a movie's going to do. Look at Josh Groban. His music was in *Troy*, which was going to be the biggest movie that ever happened. My music was in *Down With Love*, which was supposed to be this huge movie. Renée Zellweger had just come off winning the Oscar. Ewan McGregor had just come off *Moulin Rouge*.

'I enjoyed the movie, but commercially it didn't enjoy the success people thought it would. If I can get my music in there, I think it's a great thing. [Movies are] really just another great form of promotion. I think it's more important for me to actually take the time to tour, to show up and be tangible to my audiences in the twenty-odd countries. If I start concentrating on acting or soundtracks, I start leaving out valued customers who have been good enough to spend their hard-earned money to buy my product.' And while Michael might have been thinking of the strategic consequences for his own career, that comment displayed a degree of concern for his fans, which he was to display over and again in the next few years. He certainly displayed a healthy respect for the value of money – but unusually, not just the value of his own.

It must have been sweet revenge towards the industry that had ignored him for so long when Michael discovered that his early, independent records were now selling on eBay for up to $300, and they were also being used for commercial ends.

But Michael was beginning to discover the more problematic areas of fame, too. DRG Records realised that the star of the film *Totally Blonde* had suddenly turned into a famous singer, and so in 2004 released a CD of the seven songs Michael had sung in the film under the title *Totally Bublé*, which made it look like a new offering, rather than part of the soundtrack from the film. Michael was not happy about this: it was not his choice, not an official Michael Bublé CD, but there was nothing he could do about it, something he put on his website to warn off fans. He was becoming a valuable commodity now – to other people, as well as himself.

Lewis and Amber, meanwhile, perhaps aware that their eldest child was now so big a star that he was totally overshadowing the rest of the family, were always careful to make sure that the girls got a look in, too. They emphasised the fact that the baby of the family, Crystal, was an actress, regularly appearing on *Cold Squad*, while their middle child Brandee had become a special needs teacher. She had also married a man with a surname as unusual as her own. 'Can you believe she went from Bublé to Ubels when she got married?' Lewis asked. 'One funny name to another.' It was clear that the Bublé parents wanted all three of their children to know they were special, not just their very famous son.

Not that Michael was behaving in a big-headed way to those he knew best. But he was beginning to see another downside of fame. It was not conducive to relationships. Women were throwing themselves at him now and Michael didn't always throw them back, despite the fact that he was in a long-term relationship. Unsurprisingly, perhaps, that relationship began to suffer. Ultimately it was to founder altogether under the weight of Michael's career, but for now, at least, it was causing everyone involved a lot of anguish. Could Michael, the singer of a thousand love songs, actually maintain the romance in his own life? Perhaps one day – but certainly not with his first big love. His relationship with the actress Debbie Timuss was about to end in tears.

4

Down With Love

The year was 1996. Michael Bublé was an up-and-coming young singer – up-and-coming in the sense that while it was generally accepted he had talent by the yard, no one in the wider world appeared to have realised this and no one was paying him a blind bit of notice. He was still working the clubs, taking on a few dead-end acting roles, and generally getting nowhere. But there was one consolation. He was about to embark on his first serious relationship – so serious that he came close to marrying her. The woman in question was Debbie Timuss, an actress. And they were to be together a full eight years.

Like her boyfriend-to-be, Debbie came from Vancouver. She was a beauty, with long legs frequently showcased by her dancing, and very attractive to men. The couple first became friendly when both were appearing in *Red Rock Diner*, in which Michael played Elvis: indeed, Debbie, the more experienced dancer of the two, taught Michael the choreography for the show. (This also helped him in later years: 'They [the musical shows] taught me discipline and helped me with movement on stage because I had to dance a lot,' he once said.) A friendship followed, which went on to become a full-blown relationship. They were to be an established couple for years, until a combination of Michael's fame and womanising finally broke the relationship up.

But those were to be years of gigantic change, not least in the power balance between the two of them, and Michael ended up a very different person at the end of the relationship from the one he had been at the beginning. When they first met, he was hardworking and possibly a little bit naïve; by the time of the final split, he was a huge name in show business but also slightly chastened. On top of that, the couple met when they were still in their teens. It would have been surprising indeed, especially given how young they were when they first met, if their relationship had been able to withstand that.

When they first met, although Michael was working fairly constantly, Debbie was probably the more successful of the two. Indeed, there were times when it was she who was paying the rent and the bills: there was certainly no sign that she'd set up home with a budding superstar. Michael remembered the start of their relationship well. 'I had come from the clubs and I was a dangerous young man,' he told one interviewer after he became famous (and before the couple split up). 'I was the bad boy and she was the good girl about to be married, actually. I stole her from her fiancé and now someone will steal her from me soon.' That's not quite how it happened, although he was right that the romance was not to last. Nor, if truth be told, was he quite as dangerous as he made himself out to be.

Michael was not, in fact, massively experienced with

women when he met Debbie. 'I didn't lose my virginity until quite late,' he told one interviewer in 2007. 'I wasn't this great Romeo or anything at all. I didn't really get the girl, unless it was through my singing.' Even then, it didn't necessarily work out. 'Certainly when I was younger, I was quite goofy,' he said. 'I'd sing in clubs and it's true that if you have something special, it elevates you socially and you attract more attention, you're not just a dork among dorks. But I think when they were alone with me, they were a bit let down.' That was quite an admission for a heartthrob, but Michael was being realistic. At the very beginning, at least, he didn't have a lot of success with girls.

That began to change after he met Debbie. Michael developed a certain degree of maturity from the sheer experience of being in a relationship that he hadn't had before. Also, now he'd finally got started, he started at the top: Debbie was an acknowledged beauty, quite the girl any man about town would want to have on his arm.

For a while it worked. Both young and ambitious, they settled into the relationship, happy with each other and both intent on following their dream. Two years into their relationship, the duo moved to Toronto to work on *Forever Swing*, and decided to stay for a while. Toronto was a bigger city than Vancouver and so the chances of making it for either of them seemed to be all the greater. And in these early days of Michael's career, everything between the two of them was just fine. They were young and struggling to make it. Michael might have got pretty dispirited at times, but there was a romantic angle to two young, attractive people, understanding each other's predicament and being there for one another. And then came Michael's breakthrough. Everything changed.

For the first time in his life, Michael had women throwing

themselves at him. He was a bona fide star and the more successful he got, the more interested in him women became. Having never been the sought-after young stud in his teen years, this was intoxicating stuff. In his bid to make his breakthrough, after meeting up with David Foster and finally beginning to experience real success, he had also been afforded plenty of opportunity to stray: he was travelling all over the world to promote the album *Michael Bublé*, meeting fans after the gigs, and was high on the excitement of finally achieving the life he had spent so many years working for. Michael was a young man, provided with the kind of temptations few young men in his position would have been able to resist. And he didn't.

And so began the only time in Michael's life that he later looked back on with some embarrassment. Hand-in-hand with his cheating on Debbie came a certain degree of arrogance as Michael let it all go to his head. In fairness this period didn't last long, but it gave rise to a reputation for womanising and ego that in some ways still persists to this day. The reality is that he is, on the whole, quite self-deprecating, with a robust sense of humour. The image (and for a short time, also the reality) is that he would nail anything that moved.

For a start, Michael began taking full advantage of the women who threw themselves at him. The more famous he got, the more women there were who wanted to bed him, and he duly obliged. This, along with his record sales, made him begin to feel like a real hot shot. Michael Bublé briefly became, by his own account, not a nice person to know. All those women who wanted to sleep with him and all those people out there buying his albums couldn't be wrong, seemed to be the thinking. He started to believe in his own publicity and looking back on it, he was very lucky indeed that he didn't completely lose his way.

'When I started to enjoy success as a singer, I began to get cocky because it's easy to lose touch with reality in this business,' he said with a degree of honesty also frequently not found in the business. 'I would be in a police car being escorted through a crowd of screaming girls, and booze and drugs were all there for me if I wanted it. I had a girlfriend I cared a lot about, but for a while I pushed her aside and said, "This is my time. I'm going to go and do my thing." I started to be reckless with people's feelings. I felt I could be rude and say things with no comeback.'

It was not only Debbie who was dismayed: so, too, were Michael's family, friends and business associates. They did not like to see their boy behaving like such a clown and they let him know it, too. 'When I got to be a bit of a prick-head, my mom called me one day and said, "Did you get better looking or more charming this year?"' Michael admitted. 'And I said, "I don't know," and she said, "No, asshole, you didn't." They definitely keep me grounded.' Michael was fortunate indeed that his family took this attitude: his parents were thrilled that their son was finally making it, rather less so that it was so very much going to his head. Again, in part, this seemed to be some kind of overreaction against the person Michael had been at school. He'd never been the cool guy who got the girls: now he was and he wanted to make sure everyone knew about it. 'I was getting into the partying and doing everything, but in moderation I might add,' he continued.

For one of the major ironies about Michael's singing career is that while it got him the girls in his twenties, it did the opposite when he was at school. For all the talk of being influenced by the girls drooling over pictures of Harry

Connick Jr, Michael's music set him apart. Most teenagers were not, in the mid-1990s, at least, interested in the music of Frank Sinatra and Dean Martin, and for Michael to set himself up as so slavish a follower seemed a little odd. That is why Michael was so keen to emphasise that whatever he sang, he wasn't trying to be a throwback to the 1950s. 'You can try and trick the people and me come out wearing a fedora and tux, but that's not me,' he said in one interview. 'I was born in the late seventies, I wear jeans. I don't hang out in casinos. The lifestyle isn't my thing. I don't drink martinis and I don't smoke cigars.' In other words, he was a man of his own time, not a nerd who was pretending to be something he wasn't. It is an attitude that has come out in his interviews again and again.

In another interview, he compounded this impression that he was making up for the teen years. 'I lost it a little bit,' he said. 'I lost my way. I started to believe the stuff. I thought to myself: "Gosh, I can't be so nice." I had friends in the business who were more edgy and people in the press liked them more.' Certainly, bad behaviour made the news far more than politeness – although Michael was going to discover that, too, to his cost.

Why did he act like an idiot? Because he could. There was certainly no shortage of other people who were equally childish and arrogant in the world in which he now moved: Michael saw all this and took it on board a little too much. Whose behaviour was he emulating? He wouldn't say.

To be fair to him, it wasn't really Michael. Whatever he did, the real Michael was a man who adored his family and put them at the very centre of his life, who loved his parents and let them know that all the time. Indeed, if the real Michael was half the jerk he appeared to be at this time, he would never have snapped out of it. But the real Michael was, underneath it all, a nice guy who was appreciating that after all this time, he'd finally made it. The real Michael went on to become ashamed that this phase had ever come about.

It was an isolated incident that made him finally wake up. In fact, Michael's bad-boy period did not last that long and didn't really hurt anyone, but he was making a pain of himself and it was a relief to his friends and family when he finally wised up. 'It came to a head when I was on an airplane and was rude to a flight attendant,' he said. 'It wasn't the real me, but I did it. My tour manager, who has worked with much better than me, took me aside. He said, "Young man. I have met your mother and father. And I know you were raised to be much more classy a person." I thought, "Yeah, sure." Then I sat on a five-hour flight and had time to stew. I was so mad, but I had time to think. I prayed, please God help me find my way. I realised he was right and that fame is a fantasy and when it is all gone and fans aren't screaming, what would be left? My family and the girl who stuck with me for five years when I struggled and had nothing.'

It could have been worse, as Michael conceded on another occasion. He was, after all, old enough to realise what he had been doing and to calm down again before making a real idiot of himself. But that incident on the plane clearly had hit home. Michael explained afterwards that he had had expensive suits in his bag and had asked, '"Could you hang these suits?" because they were going to get creased, and she felt I was being rude . . . stupid things like that.' He continues: 'I always say, "If I was twenty-one and this [success] happened, I would have been a nightmare."'

In later years, Michael has appeared to be a little embarrassed about his behaviour, especially where women were concerned. While not making any secret of the fact that he enjoyed the attention of groupies and various other fans, in retrospect he realised, perhaps, that his behaviour wasn't very cool. 'I was never sleazy,' he told one interviewer. 'I was never mean to a girl. I was always very upfront. But I'm a regular guy. I am a lad and I did enjoy temptations.'

Debbie handled the situation with remarkable maturity. After all, she could see how famous Michael was becoming, and, working in the world of show business herself, was well aware of the temptations on offer in that world. But it was an impossible situation for her, and she let Michael know it, too. 'She didn't get mad,' he related. 'She said, "I understand what you're going through. And you must understand how embarrassing it is for me." Which made me feel like crap, you know, like, "Is it worth it?"'

And so, the couple split for a time. Debbie was well aware what was really going on and although she might have understood the temptations Michael was having to deal with, she understandably didn't feel she had to hang around to have her nose rubbed in it all. This also played a part in bringing Michael back to his senses: Debbie was, after all, his first long-term relationship, and they had been together for years. It was also Debbie who had stood by him in the lean years, who supported him sporadically when he couldn't get enough work, and who kept faith that her boyfriend was one day going to make it. She deserved considerably better than this, and Michael knew it, too. Was it really worth casting that aside for a few meaningless flings and the chance to show off?

Ultimately, the answer turned out to be 'No.' And, having reverted to his normal, charming and self-deprecating self, the first thing that Michael did was to try to make amends with Debbie. So he returned to Canada to woo back his first great love, an endeavour in which he was successful, convinced, now, that she really was the woman he wanted to spend his life with. Marriage was now being discussed. 'I've won back her love,' he cooed to one interviewer. 'She was cool and sort of understood. We're strong now and it is nice to have that security. I will get married and I want kids, but I wouldn't have time for them just now.' That was true enough, but it was also Michael harking back to the values he grew up with. A nice kid, from a Catholic immigrant family, of course he wanted to get married and have kids. It was what he'd grown up with. It was the most important aspect of life.

In fairness, Michael certainly realised in retrospect quite how overblown his ego had become. It wasn't just his relationship with Debbie that suffered: he had been, as he admitted, an idiot. A philanderer who had let it all go to his head. He also realised in the longer term how fortunate he was to have friends and family around him to bring him back to earth.

'If I didn't have the people around me, it would have been easy to lose my way,' he continued. 'I have seen celebrities act way out of line, and be mean lots of times. I was with a famous actor, who I won't name. We were hanging out having a beer at a hotel when a guy came to clean the pool. The guy said, "Hey, I enjoy your films." The actor just said, "Get the fuck out of here." I was embarrassed because I thought it was disgraceful. The pool guy just walked away and kept his dignity. It made me think of my grandfather who is a plumber. If somebody said that to him, I'd have killed them. I was like, "He's more important than you. What have you done? Made a few silly films." In my case, I was fortunate that I had great people around me – my family, management and tour manager.'

His parents took notice of that and were greatly relieved to have their son back. 'He's talking about some people who were sitting by his pool and when the pool man came and began treating him [badly],' said Amber to one interviewer, showing them the relevant article. 'Michael [hates] people like that, so he kicked them out. I wish he hadn't have sworn in the article though.' You can't have everything. Her son used fruity language. But at least he was acting like himself again.

Michael did put some thought into what had made him act in the way he did, and in fairness, there was a lot in what he said. 'You get self-absorbed, not out of evil but out of necessity, surviving that life,' he remarked. 'Then when you come home it's hard to break that off and sit down with everyone else, because you're used to doing what you want to do, when you want to do it. You know what? There've been times when I have looked in the mirror and said get over yourself.'

Now that Michael was reunited with Debbie, he wanted to make sure that that was it: they would not be parting again. Perhaps the time to get married really was now. And so he chose Valentine's Day to propose to his girlfriend, although as he tells it, matters quickly descended into farce. Michael picked a ring out in secret and had it sent to New York: disaster struck. 'I had the ring FedExed and it sat in LA customs for a bit, then they sent it to New York,' he related some time afterwards. 'I took her out for dinner and drove her crazy because she thought I was going to ask her and I didn't. Then I had the hotel room filled with blooms of flowers while we were out. We got into the room, I went to grab the box with the ring in it, I opened it up and realised it had been stolen. It got stolen at LA customs. That's what happens when you pay a guy five dollars an hour. So I went out, bought her a pair of earrings that night and two weeks later, when I got home and picked up the ring, we were in the kitchen and I said, "Here it is, baby."' It seems the ring had been stolen from the box, which had been sent on to New York, but after reporting the theft, the piece of jewellery was tracked down and Michael was able to present it to his fiancée, at last.

They were formally engaged – but tellingly, no date had yet been set. Also, although Michael reported, 'She thinks the whole music thing is a crock of shit, which I like,' he was taking his career pretty seriously, and might have been secretly hoping his girlfriend would, too. There were signs, looking back on it, that the relationship was not going to survive after all, but for now Michael was simply happy that the two were a couple once more.

A further sign that the relationship was back on course for now came in the song 'Home', on Michael's second album, *It's Time*. He actually co-wrote it himself, with one of David Foster's daughters, Amy Foster-Gillies, who was a songwriter based in Nashville, Tennessee. It was inspired by his absences from Debbie – 'May be surrounded by a million people, I still feel all alone, Just wanna go home, Oh I miss you, you know, Let me go home . . .' It turned out to be a massive hit, with Debbie singing backing vocals and appearing on the accompanying video, and it also went down well with a world hooked on romance. Somehow, that Michael should write such an emotive song to his one true love fitted in very well with his reputation as a reformed ladies' man who had seen the error of his ways: it did his reputation no harm at all. Of course, he had to keep singing it in the wake of the break-up as well – but somehow he always got through.

It was also a new, and very important, area for him in that the song was self-penned. Although he had sung some of his original material to David Foster on the fateful occasion when they first met, Michael was very much known for his covers. But he had shown signs, at times, of wanting not only to sing brand-new songs, but to create the music himself.

He found that he enjoyed it, too. 'People assume that you can take a standard and sing it over again – it's not easy,' he said. 'For the most part I am taking these songs and conceptually giving them a brand new life and feel. Let's say I cover a song like "That's Life" or "Wonderful Tonight", the Clapton song. The second it comes out, people compare it. Is it as good as Sinatra's version or Clapton's version or Dean Martin's version or [Bobby] Darin's version or [Ella] Fitzgerald's version or [Mel] Tormé's version? To make your version stand out, or at least stand on its own, it had better be interesting and have some originality. But with one of my original songs – who the hell are they going to compare it to?' Indeed.

Thanks to his success, Michael's relationship with Debbie was turning into a classic 'A Star Is Born' scenario. Debbie had been far and away the more successful of the couple when they first met and throughout most of their relationship to date: now, however, Michael was overtaking her. This led to a shift in the power balance, to say nothing of problems incurred by the sheer weight of his growing fame. If he was so much as pictured with a girl, speculation immediately had the two of them as a couple, something that could prove problematic for everyone concerned.

Michael was finding that the attitude of the press differed from country to country. As he said in one interview of the paparazzi in England, 'If I come out of a restaurant, they'll be sitting there and I'll shake their hand and say, "What do you want the picture of?" I'm really co-operative with them and they're appreciative of that.'

He was to find to his cost that the English press was not uniformly so easy to deal with, and in Italy it was already a different story. 'You'll see them with their cameras – they'll hide them in their jackets – and I'll come out and say, "Hey guys, let's do the photos and leave me alone,"' Michael continued. 'They'll say "We don't know what you talk about." They try to get you to fight them. They follow you everywhere and there's nothing you can do. The other day I was with a couple of girls from my record company and I was sitting next to one of them at dinner. Later on, her boyfriend called and said, "What's going on? What's up between you and Michael Bublé?" She was like, "What are you talking about?" The paparazzi had pictures of us having dinner. Of course, there was a table of twelve of us but I was sitting beside her and they're saying "Michael Bublé's Roman girlfriend".'

Debbie continued to cope, but it was sometimes difficult. She was with Michael when an interviewer asked him about the swooning women: 'What?' she said. 'You?' But she did concede that it caused problems. 'I have my moments,' she said. 'I think the lucky thing is we've known each other for so long. He's good. He makes an effort to make sure it's all good.'

But it wasn't. The previous infidelity had been too public, and that must have continued to hurt Debbie, no matter how much she struggled to forgive and forget about it all. And the strains and stresses were not going away. The gaps between when the two of them were able to see each other were turning out to be too long. Michael clearly did love Debbie, but he was at a stage in his life where carrying on with the relationship was just too difficult. And so, in November 2005, after an engagement that had lasted nearly a year, but had never ended up with a wedding date, the romance was finally off, once and for all.

It was a blow. For all the earlier displays of arrogance and for all the fact they both knew it was over now, they had been together for years – and those years had been, initially, the years of struggle. Only the two of them knew how difficult it had been to start out, and that creates a bond, no matter what happens over time. But why did it finally end? 'I was working. She was working,' said Michael some years later, after he'd got together with his second serious girlfriend, Emily Blunt. 'It got to be that we were never together and so we grew apart. Facing up to that was pretty crushing for both of us. And the fact is, I love her still, as much as I ever did. You don't just write someone out of your life when they've meant so much to you. There'll always be a loyalty there. Yes, I'm in love again and have this beautiful girl who I'm mad for. But there remains a place in my heart for Debbie and I'd be there for her if ever the chips were down. Emily understands that luckily and cares similarly about guys with whom she has been involved in the past.'

There were various ramifications to this. The first, and most obvious, was that Michael's song 'Home' was widely known to have been written to his first great love, from whom he had now split. Being a huge hit, however, he was still expected to perform it, and so he did. 'At first it was weird,' he said. 'It was really tough and emotional. It's a very autobiographical song. It was art imitating life imitating art.'

After one performance, he was told that he didn't quite look as if his heart was really in it. 'That can happen,' he continued, explaining that he somehow summoned the resources to sing the song without brooding on what it had once meant to him. 'You can protect yourself. We'd had a long relationship and it had just ended. But I'm glad I got through it.'

And there was an upside: like a true artist, Michael was able to turn his pain into his art. When his third album, *Call Me Irresponsible*, was released in 2007, it contained a song called 'Lost'. Again inspired by his ex, this time Michael was mourning the loss of a relationship that was no more. 'When I wrote "Lost", I was really very emotional – I was in the process of ending a relationship of eight years,' he explained when the album came out. 'I was really bummed and I felt so badly for both of us for all we'd gone through, and that it didn't work the way we'd hoped it would. I wanted "Lost" to be an anthem for all of us who have been in relationships where we loved the person and it just didn't work out – and that doesn't mean we're going to discard them from our life just because it didn't work out romantically.'

Indeed, Michael and Debbie maintained their friendship: when he'd finished writing the song, he got in touch with his ex and played it to her: 'I can't believe it's over, I watched the whole thing fall . . .' 'She bawled her eyes out,' said Michael sombrely. 'It was a tribute to us. It would be really callous of me to pretend this history didn't happen.'

Indeed, he was sounding thoroughly sentimental about it now. 'I loved the girl,' Michael continued. 'And I'll always love the girl. We just happened not to be right together, and we moved on. It was devastating. I mean, this was my best friend, you know?' She was, indeed, a huge part of his past, and there is no question that the split was devastating for both of them. But it had to be.

And there was one consolation. Michael's broken heart did good business. 'Lost' was released as a single, and although it only got to number ninety-seven on the US *Billboard* Hot

100, it reached twenty-five in Canada, fifteen in Italy and nineteen in the UK. Michael performed it on *The X Factor* in December 2007, and it also featured in an episode of *NCIS* called 'Heartland', as Agent Gibbs left the town of Stillwater and recalled how he met his first wife. And for Michael, it was time to move on. Many more areas to conquer lay ahead.

5

Men Behaving Badly

When Michael was first starting out, he was, in many ways, very naïve. Despite the fact that he'd spent years in the business, he'd had relatively few dealings with the press until finally hitting the big time, for the simple reason that no one had any interest in who he was or what he did. He was not, initially, criticised in the press for the way he was behaving. And given that his breakthrough had been so fast and so sudden, the comment he attracted initially tended towards the very positive. Because he was so young, happy and enjoying himself so much, everyone found it totally charming: rather than inspiring envy, as fame and success so often does, people actually felt pleased for him. In some ways, Michael came across as a loveable puppy. It didn't occur to him at first that there could be a downside to all this.

And when he finally did make his breakthrough, Michael didn't realise what the press might enjoy writing about, especially the British press, who have a reputation for enjoying baiting celebrities. Those friendly photographers, who were perfectly charming if he would just give them the picture they needed, were entirely typical. In short, Michael was so used to receiving positive coverage that the alternative seemed unthinkable. But he was playing an increasingly dangerous game: his behaviour by now was getting more cheeky, and someone was bound to notice it eventually. And on top of that, Michael made one very big mistake: he thought the journalists were his friends.

It was an easy mistake to make. Michael was young and personable and so were the journalists he was hanging out with. Why shouldn't he have a little fun? And if he was on tour in the company of journalists, and they were all hanging out together, surely there was no problem in letting his hair down a little when the microphone had been switched off, right? Wrong.

What Michael hadn't realised was that he was by now well and truly in the public eye, and when that happens, different rules apply. He simply couldn't go for a fun night out with the boys, chat to women and be one of the lads – not if one of those lads was a journalist. Michael had turned into a news story, potential good copy. And while he went on to own up to all his indiscretions pretty bravely, at that stage he simply didn't understand what could – and did – happen next. It was a salutary lesson and one he is unlikely to forget.

It was early 2004 and Michael was on tour in the Philippines. With him was the journalist Michael Odell, who went on to write up a profile of his namesake for the April 2004 issue of Q magazine. It caused an absolute sensation, in that it purported to be a behind-the-scenes exposé of what Michael Bublé was supposedly like.

With spectacularly bad timing, Michael and Debbie had

just got back together when the article appeared. She was not pleased, not one little jot. 'I was very upset, yes,' she told one interviewer. 'We'd gotten back together when it came out. It was a very bad time. But he admits it and says he's learned his lesson.' It was another step in his rehabilitation. If his girlfriend was ready to forgive him, then why should the rest of the world pay any attention?

Not that everyone was so appalled anyway: some seemed to be taking it rather well. Michael was having to put up with the reactions of the people around him who were managing his career: they were all older than him, had been around a good deal longer and had seen it all before. They knew the storm would blow over and that it might even be a good thing to have happened if it made Michael aware that he'd been behaving unwisely. Bruce Allen, if anything, appeared amused. 'Well, it shows he's certainly not packaged,' he said. That was indeed true. Liz Rosenberg, who now did much of Michael's publicity, remarked that it was youthful excess, and given that Michael was still only in his late-twenties, there was certainly something in that. And in a way, it was a shame that it provoked Michael into being so very much more cautious in the future: so many stars these days will not speak without a PR present, copy approval and the works. If nothing else, Michael was a breath of fresh air.

But this interview did make him cautious. He learned the lesson that everyone in the public eye finds out eventually: the journalist is not necessarily someone to open up to. Although that trademark honesty still came through, along with a certain ruefulness, he was now exhibiting a wariness around journalists he had never shown before, telling one interviewer, 'I'm very afraid of you' – hardly surprising, given the mauling his reputation had just received. 'The British press are so classy, aren't they?' he went on. 'I learned my lesson. I learned that the writers are not your friends.' He could say that again. Writers were out there looking for a story, and Michael was well and truly it.

It was perhaps not surprising that it was with the British press that Michael's fingers were so well and truly burned. North American newspapers and magazines tend to be far worthier than their British counterparts, while the British press does have a habit of knocking celebrities down a peg or two. Michael was certainly not alone in experiencing a certain amount of discomfort at their hands, but it was also embarrassing, given that he was beginning to accumulate a sizeable fan base in Britain. It might have been a sharp learning curve, but that didn't make it any better or make him any less upset.

And it cast that aspect of his life in a different light, too. Pre-Q magazine, Michael had thought that journalists were interested in his life story, the kid from a working-class family who'd made good, as well as his thoughts about the music he made. Now he realised that at least some of them were quite happy to try and make him look ridiculous. It seems a little odd that no one at his record company had pointed out these potential pitfalls, although it was perfectly possible that at that stage Michael would simply have refused to listen. But it had still been a very unpleasant time. 'It ruined me and it ruined the interviewing experience for me,' he said. 'For so many others now, I am so careful. I'd rather almost say nothing. But I like to say what I want to say, and I was never mean to anybody.' Indeed.

In fact, there was no chance at all he was going to say nothing. He'd made a stupid mistake, that was for sure. But hey. Nobody was dead. Michael was – is – an earthy character and so, even when his subject matter was slightly more profound than the charms of the ladies, he couldn't help still sounding a little juicy, as when he was musing on the subject of fulfilment. 'Happiness in life doesn't come from achieving your goals, but from dreaming of your potential, of looking forward to something,' he said. 'Let's say there's a beautiful woman. You must have her because she's the greatest thing you've ever seen and you court her and you charm her and you work so hard to have her. Then you get her and four days later you're bored. You show me a beautiful woman and I'll show you a guy who's tired of screwing her.' Well, as was increasingly obvious – he should know.

But Debbie was right: at the heart of his character was not malice, but goofiness. Journalists – and anyone else – who met him were sometimes taken aback to discover quite what colourful language he used, but then, why shouldn't he? His background, after all, was as a fisherman, and fishermen are known to be earthy characters whose language can sometimes get a little ripe. Michael was simply reflecting what he knew best and the way he was brought up. He was certainly not out to harm.

And anyway, he was making a lot of people very happy with his music. Michael had a tour to do and was still explaining to his rapidly growing fan base what made his own particular style. There was intense curiosity about him musically, as much as in every other way, and about the image that he exuded. Did he want to adopt the mantle of Sinatra? Yes and no. 'I think people expect me to come out in a tuxedo, smoking a cigar with a Scotch in my hand, saying: "It's a pleasure to be here. How did you all get in my room?"' he said in an interview that appeared shortly before the Q magazine debacle. 'But I'm young, I'm immature, I'm a punk. I'm everything that a good young man should be.' Q magazine briefly put paid to that one, but the point was made once again. Michael was not a throwback: he was living in the here and now.

Just as he had done in the past, Michael continued to be very keen to emphasise that whatever the music he sang, he was basically a regular guy. Despite the fact that he was now so famous, his desire to distance himself from the ribbing he'd received as a youngster appeared to be stronger than ever, and that meant laying claim to some street cred. At the same time, however, for the first time, he seemed to be saying that actually, given half a chance, his peers would have done what he had done.

Indeed, nothing could compare with the greats and he wasn't afraid to say so. Michael played an interviewer Frank Sinatra's *Live at the Sands*, with the Count Basie Orchestra and arranged and conducted by Quincy Jones: as far as he was concerned, it was beyond compare. 'Does it get any better?' he asked. 'I don't think so. Here we have Sinatra in his prime. Just hear his tone, his vibrato and picture his cocksure swagger as he's walking on stage and you will understand why there will never be another like him. Listening to this made me learn that I could never try to imitate him, and, to be honest, Elvis Presley and Bryan Adams have been far bigger influences. Frank was just a man with a great voice who sang the songs I liked.'

There was another reason for this constant desire to distance himself from the great Sinatra: given that Ol' Blue Eyes was one of the greatest performers of the twentieth century, Michael knew that if it looked as if he were inviting comparisons, he was almost certainly setting himself up for a fall. It would have been incredibly foolish to present himself as the anointed heir to that particular crown: there was only one Sinatra, and the younger generation, as well as the older one, wouldn't take too kindly to a young pretender trying to muscle his way in. Much better to do what he was doing: presenting himself as a modern guardian of music that had been passed down through generations, as well as a man of his own time.

However, Michael's relationship with his music was not entirely straightforward. His attitude frequently came across as ambivalent. Was he slightly embarrassed about having been so different in his tastes from the other kids when growing up? The more famous he got, the less so he appeared. 'When I was growing up, this music was everywhere,' he said on one visit to the UK in 2004. 'I'd hear it at home, in coffee shops, commercials. Of course, I heard modern stuff too – Nirvana and Pearl Jam – but while there was melody there, it wasn't enough for me. All I can tell you about this music can be summed up in one word: melody.' Poor Kurt Cobain, Nirvana's lead singer – downgraded very quickly after the previous occasion on which Michael had talked about him. But Michael wasn't through.

'In a way, this was my rebellion,' he continued. 'When I was growing up, kids weren't given any choice. Radio stations and record companies weren't servicing people who weren't between thirteen and sixteen. They took every bit of shit for that demographic and threw it at them.'

He did, however, emphasise over and over that he was not trying to emulate the greats: he was trying to present the old songs in a new light. He had colossal stage presence, too, teasing his audience, flirting with them, encouraging them to get up and dance. When Michael came on, you knew about it. How much of it was him and how much was put on?

'There's an element of an act, but that's an extension of any performer,' he explained. 'Someone once told me I wasn't old enough to sing about heartbreak, but I said, "If an actor has to play a junkie, does he have to take heroin?" Look, I was not born in 1930 and I am not nostalgic about this music. I don't drink martinis and I'm not Frank Sinatra. Frank was great, but Frank's dead. I'm Michael Bublé.' Indeed, in comments like this one, there was a real sense of frustration that people kept comparing him to the greats of another age. This was his age, now, and he wanted to be seen as a modern singer. The reaction to him could sometimes be frustrating stuff.

It was a pretty stout defence of his work and he got annoyed when people felt the music he played was bland, too. Indeed, sometimes it seemed as if people were intent on finding anything at all they could to criticise, and Michael sometimes sounded a little fed up. 'For too long there were a lot of people being left out of the loop,' he said. 'I like rap, pop and R&B. I can hear it's good but for too long there has only been room for that and no room for . . . I don't want to call it easy listening because easy listening is not what I do.' The term easy listening was, indeed, one that was often used as an insult. Totally meaningless anyway, easy listening was just another label, and Michael was fed up with people who wanted to put him in one particular box.

It was an odd position to be in: a modern young man constantly compared to people who were in their heyday thirty years earlier. And yet he coped. He coped with the other elements of his new stardom, too. As the repercussions of the Q magazine article began to die down, Michael continued to be honest about his recent past. 'I'm crooning, they're swooning,' he declared of his fans in another magazine interview, but there was a degree of self-realisation now that hadn't been there before. 'Yeah, I've slept with fans. But there's a sad real-isation when you think, I'm a celebrity, that's why.'

That was a self-aware comment. Michael might have been deluding himself that all the women who threw themselves at him wanted him for his personality and the in-depth nature of his soul, but the truth was he – like them – could have been anyone. The only difference was that in his case, the other anyones would have had to have been as rich and famous as he was. For all that Michael might have been using the women, absolutely as much applied in the other direction. It is one of the strange quirks of modern celebrity, that while famous men might get their pick of women and end up using them as commodities, pretty much exactly the same happens in reverse.

Michael was beginning to learn that. He had a pretty good sense of humour about it, as well. He might be irresistibly attractive to women these days, but he knew why, and he was also capable of seeing how idiotic it could all sometimes be. 'Once I had a teddy bear sent to me,' he confided. 'I planned to give it to my nephew. Then I pressed its paw and a woman's voice said, "Hi, this is Henrietta. I want to touch you. I'm staying at this hotel . . ."' But although that degree of honesty remained, he was being far more careful about what he said in public. It looked like he was growing up.

But he wasn't going to shut up about everything. Michael's people were right: he wasn't packaged and he con-tinued to come out with comments that might have caused a little shock. His use of dope was one of them: Michael had always been totally honest about smoking joints and despite being warned that it might raise eyebrows, he refused to pretend it wasn't a part of him. 'There was a time when I told a journalist I might have had a bit of a joint once,' he announced. 'Some people told me not to admit to things like that as I could alienate a section of my audience. You know, I thought about that for a few days. But then I decided that I only want to have real fans; people who are into me for what I am.'

It is a mark of how successful Michael now was that he genuinely thought that: a few years previously, the thought that he might have a fan base at all, let alone one that might be offended, would have stunned him and might even have curbed his tongue. Now, he could say that people could take him or leave him precisely because so many people were doing the former. And he returned to the subject of dope more than once. 'Actually, I'm not into drink as much as into puffing,' he told another journalist (he was certainly different from his Rat Pack forebears there). 'I don't know any man who's smoked cannabis and then gone home and beaten his wife.'

Eventually, though, professional pressures were to force him to cut back on smoking joints – not because anyone disapproved, but because there was a real danger it would begin to affect his voice. As he told one interviewer, 'I like to smoke what you call a spliff. If it was up to me, I'd walk through life in a haze. But I had to stop all of that because it kills your voice. Three hundred shows in a year, man, and sometimes I'd show up and be half as good as I should have been. I felt bad about that.'

Indeed, he was now having to look after himself in a way he had never done before. Michael could get a little chubby if he wasn't careful: he was now talking about high protein, low carb diets and how well they worked. He had to keep an eye on himself, watch what he ate and go to the gym. Where once those tough summers on his father's boat would have been more than enough to keep up his fitness levels, these days he lived a considerably more comfortable life in which just about anything he wanted was there for the taking, and that included food.

Michael was of Italian origin: he was born to love good home-cooking. But now he had to learn to say no. Even Michael, supremely unconcerned about such trivia as his appearance, was beginning to understand that other people were not so laissez-faire and that now he couldn't be, either: the public expects something of its stars. They do not want them hanging around looking like slobs, and so he was beginning to see that he had to put the various elements of his lifestyle into compartments. Pizza-loving Michael was fine when he was at home, away from the fans. The public Michael, the one on tour, on television, and out there showing what he could do, was the Michael who had to stick to high-protein shakes and salads.

He empathised with his fellow celebs on that score, too. 'The last thing I want to see is pictures of my fat ass in magazines,' he said in one revealing interview, although he couldn't resist going on to joke about it, too. 'Sometimes I open these mags and there are close-ups of a girl with unshaven armpits or looking fat on the beach. All of us get a little overweight when we are not doing promotions. When I have a month off I am going to eat pizza and watch movies and not bother about looking good. [One starlet had] printed a photograph of the actress with her breast op scar showing. That's unfortunate. That's why I'm never getting my breasts done. At least my babies are natural. With some women in Los Angeles, you hug them and it's like two bowling balls smack you in the chest.'

'All of us'! What a long way Michael had come. It had still, actually, been only one year since Michael had made his break-through, but he was living in a different world, now. Quite apart from the groupies and, indeed, the intrusive paparazzi shots, Michael, while not as rich as the likes of David Foster, was fast heading that way. His was becoming the world not just of the five-star hotel – anyone, even non-celebs, can manage that – but the private jet. The media intrusion. The awareness of image – the fact that, indeed, while he might slob around in private, he certainly couldn't do it in public.

And in that, for all his reluctance to link himself to the greats of yesterday, there was a similarity. The Rat Pack never went out looking anything less than immaculate, and Michael was beginning to do the same too. He might not have sported quite the sharp look that those masters of yesteryear did, but he had his own very distinct smile. Heck, he had his hair. Michael was beginning to perfect what you might call an artful rumpledness: look at pictures of him, and you'll see a natural young man, laughing and enjoying himself and being happy. Look again and you'll see someone who has an immac-ulately coiffed head of hair.

Meanwhile, there was his personal life. Michael had nearly given up on show business when he realised that one day he would want to marry and have children, but had to be sure he would be able to support them. That desire was still there. Who was the lucky woman to be? By now back with Debbie, he was also pretty sure about what he really wanted in a woman, and it wasn't just looks. 'I look for humility, kindness and grace,' he said. 'I can tell if she's been tucked into bed by her mum or dad as a kid. That's how I was raised, I'm very close to my family, and I like women who have the same values.' That was the real Michael Bublé speaking – at heart a family man.

That made it all the more ironic that in May 2004, when the news broke that the Irish Taoiseach Bertie Ahern's daughter Cecelia had split up with her athlete boyfriend David Keoghan, Michael's name was mentioned. Again, he was finding out the downside of celebrity: everything he did made news – even when, as in this case, he hadn't done it. But the point is that the rumour mill grew and as soon as Michael's name was thrown into the mix, it became news.

Everyone involved denied point blank that he had anything to do with the split, however, not least Cecelia. 'There have been rumours this week that Cecelia and I have split due to her friendship with the Canadian singer Michael Bublé,' said an irritable David. 'This is not true as far as I'm concerned. They met on *The Kelly Show* [a long-running entertainment programme on Irish television hosted by Gerry Kelly] eight months ago and know each other, but it is not the reason we broke up. There is no one else involved on either mine or Cecelia's side of things. She is writing her books and I am trying to qualify for this year's Olympic Games in Athens. We just grew apart like busy people do.' He was clearly annoyed that Michael's name had been dragged into it, but then by this time what Michael did made the news. Gossip, however untrue, attaches itself to mega-fame. He'd found that out with Q magazine and he was to find it out years later, too, when he once again found himself at the centre of a scandal. But he simply had to learn to cope.

That earthiness refused to go away: indeed, it was one of the features that made him such an attractive and amiable man to deal with. Whatever anyone thought about him, what you saw was what you got. None of it was put on. He enjoyed teasing people and couldn't resist telling all about the people he found attractive, too. 'I saw Dannii Minogue at the World

Music Awards and she's really hot!' he said. 'I spent some time in the UK and watched *I'm a Celebrity . . . Get Me Out of Here* and Jordan was so much cuter than I thought she'd be. You also know that you'd have more fun with Christina Aguilera than Britney Spears.' (This was not an undisputed point of view.)

Touring the UK in mid-2004, Michael was garnering excellent reviews. The shows were sellouts, with Michael himself occasionally in tears when he talked about Grandpa Mitch and how much he'd helped him. He was winning over the men in the audience as well as the women, sympathizing with them for having been dragged along by their wives and girlfriends: 'I know a lot of you gentlemen out there didn't want anything to do with this shit tonight,' he quipped, before adding that he hoped they'd 'get laid' for their trouble. It all went down a treat.

But as his career progressed, there was the minor matter of following up his own success. For all the fame and stardom, the stage manner and the increasingly confident shtick, Michael had still only had one best-selling album. There was as yet no proof positive that he was here to stay. Might he be a one-hit, or rather, one-album wonder? It was a question that was preying on his mind. What was to come next? How to follow what he had already done? These were new and difficult preoccupations of a type he'd never had to deal with before and it was no fun trying to sort it all out.

And what about his relationship with other people in the business? The older generation clearly loved him, but what about people his own age? Michael could seem a little bumptious at times: for all his many good qualities, he did not always seem brimming over with modesty. His was a competitive field and when you'd been plugging away as long as

Michael, you certainly didn't want to see others succeeding where you'd failed. Nor was he the only young man of his generation making a career for himself singing the old classics. Just how, exactly, did he get on with the rest?

6

Michael B and Jamie C

As Michael worked his way up the greasy pole, it was becoming obvious that he was not alone. Quite a few other people were making their breakthrough, singing the same kind of songs that he was. Prime among them was Jamie Cullum, another talented artist who had also gone from making self-produced albums to, in his case, performing for the Queen. And he'd appeared on Michael Parkinson's show, too.

Right from the start, the similarities between the two of them were obvious and as the two became increasingly famous, so they were increasingly spoken of in the same breath. Michael seemed to find this easier to deal with than Jamie and at least it made a change from the other comparisons the two of them had to put up with so often, with the great figures from the past. Michael might have got irritated with the constant association with Jamie and vice versa, but at least the two of them were still alive. And they, along with a few other artists, were being increasingly linked in the public consciousness, too.

That Michael Parkinson connection was relevant, for Parkinson's role was becoming more marked by this time. Way back in the heyday of his chat show in the 1970s, he had been the champion of the great jazz musicians of the day, and here he was, at it again. His resurgence as a chat-show host coincided exactly with the rise of the new jazz musicians, and the relationship between presenter and artists suited both perfectly. Indeed, Parky was becoming quite the talent spotter: an appearance on his show could set an artist up for life. He helped Michael in his British breakthrough, as well as featuring Jamie and a fair few of the other up-and-coming stars of the day.

Something was definitely going on here. Change was in the air. It wasn't just Michael Parkinson who had suddenly become relevant again: other trends were highlighting the rise of the likes of Michael and Jamie, both of whom had had to battle so many accusations of hanging on to the coat tails of the long departed greats, and both of whom were now seeming so very much like creatures of their time. Another indicator that the two were where the action was, were listening figures for the last quarter of 2003. In that three-month period, Radio 2's audience was up by 917,000, or 15.2 per cent, to 13.3 million, while Radio 1 lost 288,000 listeners, reaching only 10.5 million adults. And Michael and Jamie were a natural fit for Radio 2, not Radio 1.

'Radio 2 has always been about the excellence of the music,' said Lesley Douglas, then the station's controller, in an interview back in 2004. 'That breadth of output was based on a trust in the presenters. What we've never done is given the presenters a running order and said, "Right, that's what you're playing." What we do is manage the heart of the running order but it seems to me that my job, as Jim's was before [Jim

Moir, her predecessor], is to decide who are the right presenters, to make sure the right producers are with them and trust them.'

This independence, and the fact that the increasingly popular channels like Radio 2 did not need to feature a set playlist, aimed at the very young and of no interest whatsoever to anyone else, again benefited the likes of Michael and Jamie hugely. They probably wouldn't have got on to the playlists of Radio 1, but then, those playlists were becoming increasingly irrelevant anyway. Music was growing up; the country was growing up. The two young men and their various other counterparts were increasingly what the people wanted to hear and see. 'People have come round to our way of thinking,' Lesley Douglas said. 'The changes went by almost unnoticed. Radio 2's brand values have always remained quite constant.'

All fair comment, but of course the major factor was the fashion of the day. Radio 2 was proving itself to be more in tune with the times than Radio 1, and now a big and growing group of new entertainers were finding their new home there. But it was Michael and Jamie who were linked together more often than any other of these emerging stars. It was a double-edged sword. On the one hand, both were young, attractive and talented; on the other hand, they both wanted to be judged on their own merits and at times found it very tiresome, continually having someone else's name linked to their own. Jamie, in particular, could sound very prickly indeed.

'I'd be worried if I was put in the same category as Michael Bublé – I'm trying to sound like a young man, for starters,' he told one startled interviewer fairly soon after the pair made their breakthroughs, adding hastily, 'Michael Bublé's great, but it's a different kind of thing. It's something I'm trying to steer clear of in a way: that "recreation" of something. Michael's not really doing anything new, but what he does, he does really well.'

It was a compliment – of sorts. Jamie, incidentally, is two years younger than Michael. That was the last remark he made along those lines, at least in public, however. The press would have enjoyed nothing more than a good bullfight between the two young men, but either someone told Jamie or he worked it out for himself that it was a far better policy to praise his perceived rival; slagging Michael off could end up making Jamie look sour and bitter, especially if Michael's records sold better than his (it was a close-run thing).

Michael himself never fell into that trap. He was always polite, at the very least, and frequently effusive, about his fellow musicians. The spoilt-brat phase might have made him a little careless of the feelings of others who weren't in the industry, but entertainers coming up at the same time as he was were safe from any barbed remarks. It is possible he felt a considerable amount of empathy for them: given the amount of time he'd taken to make it, he knew how it felt to slog away at a show business career. And his natural enthusiasm and generosity to his fellow performers went down very well. 'I'm a huge fan of what Jamie brings to the music,' he said on one occasion. 'He's a cross between Harry Connick Jr and Billy Joel. We're in the same genre, but we're like The Darkness and U2 – they're both rock bands but they're very different.' It was as astute a way of putting it as anything else.

There was, however, the risk of mischief-making from other sources. Other people, both in and out of the industry, noticed the potential for rivalry, too. There were noticeboards set up on the internet to debate the duo's rival charms (it seemed to be pretty 50/50), with really quite impassioned postings about one or the other. There were rumours they both felt wary of each other (hardly surprising, given Jamie's tactlessness), so much so that in 2003, round about the time that both went into the stratosphere, they appeared on stage together. The message was plain: they were quite clearly friends.

Michael was able to laugh about it, though: when he walked on stage for a performance at Ronnie Scott's early in his British breakthrough tour, he told the audience, 'I'm just one of many people keeping this wonderful music alive.' He then introduced himself and continued, 'Oh, you know? OK, I thought you might think I was Jamie Cullum.' That was the occasion on which, later in the evening he was joined on stage by none other than Cullum himself, who was learning to be a good deal more diplomatic; the duo sang 'You Make Me Feel So Young'. (Michael changed the last word to 'hung'. That earthy, fisherman humour certainly hadn't disappeared.)

And so it went on. An article about one frequently carried a reference to the other. And the similarities were there for all to see: quite apart from the music, both were young, personable, very attractive to women, successful, and they both sang the kind of music that until recently had not been in vogue. Both somehow exuded an aura of success. Occasionally, one was mistaken for the other – but never by anyone really in the know. But it must have been trying, simply because it happened so often: in Britain, in particular, it sometimes seemed impossible to read an article about one of them without the other being dragged in. It would hardly have been surprising had it not made them a little tight-lipped.

The success of artists like Michael and Jamie still raised eyebrows in some quarters: fans of rock 'n' roll were clearly a little horrified about what was going on. Given, however, that many had believed this kind of music was very yesterday, it was really now beginning to make its mark.

Stuart Maconie is a Radio 2 presenter, an erstwhile *New Musical Express* writer, and typical of the people who were making this new (old) type of music so very popular. 'The rock and pop audience has changed,' he said. 'It isn't teenagers any more. They've grown up. Teenagers now have been brought up on what we would once call Light Entertainment, that *Pop Idol* school of thought. We were crying out for a good, specialist station. That's what Radio 2 is. What's happened here is exactly the same as what happened in music magazines in the eighties. When *Q* came along it was no longer acceptable to be sniffy or sneer at people's record collections, which is what we used to do at the *NME*. You can't say to people, "If you don't like glitzy techno then you are a failed human being," any more. You are allowed to be amicable about it. I can put on a playlisted Atomic Kitten record now and make an aside about it, because a maximum of four records an hour are playlisted for this show and the rest of it is stuff that me and the producer have chosen. The listeners learn to trust you.' All this was a way of saying that something else was going on. Tastes in music were changing and the resurgence of Radio 2 over Radio 1 was a sign of it. And Michael was surfing that wave.

It wasn't just that Michael and Jamie were hot new talents on the block: they were hot new talents who were popularising a totally different type of music from that which teenagers had listened to for years. And that was what was more noticeable than anything else: Michael and Jamie's fans were not middle-aged people, but young. For anyone who thought Nirvana was where it was at, Michael's and Jamie's success was simply inexplicable. Just how had all this come about?

Some people put the new trend down to someone else altogether: an ex-member of Take That. Robbie Williams had just released an album of old classics, *Swing While You're Winning*, introducing the old standards to a whole new audience, thus opening doors for Michael and Jamie. But they were safer than Robbie, with none of the outbursts that so characterised his life. 'Robbie Williams undoubtedly paved the way for them,' said Paul Rees, editor of Q magazine, about four months before the journal published its devastating exposé.

'They're like Robbie Williams, but with no swearing, no tattoos and no drug problems. The way a men's magazine portrays the 1950s is appealing: hard drinking, loads of women, the mob. But then these artists don't seem to embody that, do they? You can't really imagine little Jamie Cullum consorting with the mafia.' There was an unmistakable edge to his tone: Rees was clearly not one of those who approved of this new trend.

But other people were far more enthusiastic. Adam Hollywood, director of marketing at Michael's label, WEA, thought it was the music itself, with its inherent quality, that was making the pair fans. They appealed to 'the young housewife audience: women who grew up on Take That and Robbie Williams, but are now at home, listening to Radio 2,' he said. 'For years, this was a disenfranchised audience, one that was never marketed to before. Now you have powerful programmes like *Parkinson*, which can break an artist in the UK. Daytime TV is very powerful now as well. Des and Mel, Richard and Judy, *This Morning*, Terry and Gaby [Terry Wogan and Gaby Roslin, hosts of the *Terry and Gaby Show*] – those shows are aimed at women at home with disposable income, and they're full of record advertising.

'Plus there's supermarkets: five years ago, they weren't really in the game, but now as you're getting your weekly shop, you can get a bit of Bublé in your basket. Look at this week's top twenty albums. Half of them are geared towards that housewife market: Hayley Westenra, Michael Bublé, Jamie Cullum, Bryn Terfel, even Dido. It's probably easier to market this kind of artist than it is an alternative rock band now.'

This was a huge change in the nation's listening (and shopping) habits and one that was massively beneficial to both Michael and Jamie. It is impossible to say whether they became popular because of the music or the music became popular because of them, but something was happening. For whatever reason, the two were riding the crest of a wave. Many people believed the growing popularity of reality television also had something to do with it: people singing the kind of music popularised by Michael and Jamie were now appearing regularly on TV. Indeed, a fair few of them were citing Michael and Jamie as their influences. They were entering the mainstream of the musical establishment: although both were relative newcomers, they were beginning to extend an influence far beyond anything either of them had been able to do before.

Television was crucial to all this. Certainly, the Parkinson influence could not be underestimated. A personal fan of the type of music the boys played, he was championing their cause from a very powerful position indeed. His team was equally keen. 'We're music enthusiasts,' said Danny Dignan, producer of *Parkinson*, referring to himself, Parky and the show's executive producer, Bea Ballard. 'We'd already heard about Michael Bublé and Jamie Cullum long before their PR machines kicked in. He [Parkinson] went around for weeks saying the Michael Bublé album was one of the best debut albums he'd ever heard.'

Parkinson also supported Jamie on his radio show, and was responsible for the likes of various others, including Norah Jones, entering the public's consciousness, too. In this, the veteran Parky was more in tune with the nation's tastes than the edgier music critics who couldn't stand the likes of Michael and Jamie but who, for once, were simply out of tune with the times.

Michael himself was well aware of just how valuable all this, primarily his appearances on *Parkinson*, was to him. It was still very difficult to promote his music in the more traditional ways and so he needed all the exposure elsewhere that he could get. 'We don't get a lot of radio play, we don't have videos on MTV,' he said. 'I do TV shows and stuff like that and that's what sold the record, along with word-of-mouth. It's important for any artist to realise you need a great deal of support from many different places, you can't do it all yourself. Without Michael Parkinson, I fear that you in the UK would not have heard of me. He was so influential. I said to him, "It must be nice to have the power you have to help out two young guys like Jamie Cullum and myself." He just said, "You'd have done it with or without me."' Perhaps, but the Parkinson factor certainly helped.

How much did all these disparate fields feed into each other? A great deal. Michael, clearly, has a voice and a talent which is God-given, but it was apparent at this stage that luck also played a part. Singing the kind of music he did, he would almost certainly not have made it twenty years earlier. It's hard to know which came first, the chicken or the egg: did this kind of music become popular again, thus dragging up Michael and other singers in his wake, or did Michael and the others actually make it popular again? It's impossible to say. However, it was clear that everyone – the radio station, the listener and above all the performer – was benefiting from this. There was a synergy going on. Right place, right people, right tastes, right time.

Then there was the music itself, which provoked constant debate, and not just from angry young rock critics who didn't appreciate the current musical trends. Much was made of the fact that jazz was going mainstream, but even here, there was controversy. Was what Michael and Jamie were singing really jazz? If not, what were they up to? On the opposite side of the fence from people like Paul Rees were rarified jazz lovers who also didn't like what they now heard.

'Ella Fitzgerald was a great jazz artist, and she was also a very easy-listening artist, if you look at things she did like the *Great American Songbook* albums,' said Bill Holland, director of Jamie Cullum's label Universal Classics and Jazz. 'She was as much jazz – or as little – as Frank Sinatra. He started out with Tommy Dorsey's band, so you could call him jazz. The line between jazz and easy listening is very narrow. Today, a lot of people would call Michael Bublé a jazz artist, but when he sings a Bee Gees song it probably causes jazz purists to throw up their hands in horror.'

Jazz purists aside, though, it was young rock critics who really hated all of this. Michael and Jamie embodied a totally different kind of music from the type they wanted to hear and they simply couldn't understand why the two were so popular with their own generation. 'The battle of the bland,' sniped one, clearly unable to suppress his horror at the fact that both Michael and Jamie had gone platinum and were now out-selling traditional bad boy rock. This was also, of course, another reason that Michael could sometimes sound defensive when he said he didn't want to hark back to members of the Rat Pack but to bring something new to the interpretation of the music. His contemporaries in the rock press couldn't abide his songs – or his success. This might, incidentally, have played a part in the Q magazine farrago, although no one ever admitted as much.

Paul Rees certainly didn't sound as if he approved of the trend. 'Kids grow up quicker these days,' he said. 'Musically, they're more interested in blending in with their parents than rebelling against them: they look at their parents' record collection and see things like Fleetwood Mac. Ten years ago that would have been considered hopelessly uncool, now it's OK. But still, there's something fundamentally wrong about a man in his twenties wanting to sound like Dean Martin rather than Eminem, isn't there?'

Not necessarily. No one seemed to be able to pinpoint just why Michael, Jamie and co. were so popular – another theory had it that after Frank Sinatra's death in 1998, interest in the Rat Pack had blossomed to such an extent that it was affecting people's musical tastes – but the fact was that they were. Yet another reason might have been simply that the music was good. These songs, certainly the ones that Michael sang, had stood the test of time. Perhaps it was a testament to the innate quality of the lyrics, combined with their skills as entertainers, that brought Michael and Jamie such success. Above all, however, they were at the crest of the wave. Who knew how it had all come about? It just had, and they, along with their fellow entertainers, were doing very well out of it. And enjoying it, too.

Nor did it hurt the cause of either of them that both had extremely striking and attractive girlfriends. After Michael's relationship with Debbie broke up, his going on to date the British actress Emily Blunt made him even more of an aspirational figure. That he so obviously had what it took to attract some of the most beautiful women of the day did not exactly do his public image any harm. Meanwhile, Jamie was being regularly linked to the supermodel Sophie Dahl, with whom he went on to form a serious relationship. If anyone thought these two men and the others making music like them were geeks, they were in for a shock. Women like this had the pick of all the menfolk available to them, and they still chose Michael and Jamie. They were getting the seal of approval, as it were, from all sides. And that was without the record sales, and the view of the great buying public. What more could they all want?

But still rumours persisted of a rivalry between the two. Michael and Jamie seemed equally determined to prove to the rest of the world that they were friends: following Jamie's appearance onstage with Michael at Ronnie Scott's, they made frequent further appearances at each other's shows, while Michael sometimes thanked Jamie onstage for keeping the music alive and bigging him up, as it were, whenever he could. 'I'm a big fan and friend of Jamie Cullum,' he said in one interview. 'I got his CD and I thought, "Man, this is good!" We hang out when we can, he's a cool, nice guy.'

At least Jamie understood the kind of criticism Michael sometimes had to take. Like Michael, Jamie was frequently taunted as being a throwback to a bygone era, rather than a modern young product of today, despite the presence of Sophie on his arm. If Michael was the crooner, then Jamie was the jazz singer, and he was not always given an easy ride. He, too, was often compared to the old greats – 'Sinatra in sneakers' – as well as having the added burden, like Michael, of being argued over by purists. Was he a proper jazz singer or was he not?

'I love those arguments,' Jamie said, sounding much as

Michael so often did when he was called upon to defend his own music. 'I'm flattered by the attention and realise that I'm not yet a great jazz musician. But people have to understand that's what I'm striving to be – that's the lifetime project.' As with Michael, he was in it for the longer term.

Like Michael he was often forced to defend his genre. There appeared to be a perception that if you were interested in something that had started before you were born, then you were a little odd. It was a bizarre attitude to take – people were not criticised for reading books written before they arrived on the planet, but many took the view that the music Jamie espoused couldn't possibly be relevant to the twenty-something generation 'There are lots of sides to me,' he told one interviewer. 'When people ask me why I play jazz, I say that I think good music is relevant to any generation, in the way that *On the Road* was relevant to me, even though I didn't grow up in the US in the 1950s.

'I can get the same hit from "I Get a Kick Out of You" as I do from Nirvana's "Smells Like Teen Spirit". I'm from that generation and I bunked off school the day Cobain died. At that time I would have ridiculed songs like "I Get a Kick". But when I played at festivals last year, kids were coming up to me and asking: "What was that 'cocaine' song you sang?"' Shades of Bublé there as well, even citing the same band, Nirvana, to prove his modernity. It was no wonder each knew how the other felt.

Jamie Cullum also got exactly the same accusations of blandness, yet something else he had to defend himself about. 'You know, I'm fascinated by the way some critics have accused me, and artists like me, of being boring,' he said. 'These people probably go home to their wife and kids and moan about how things used to be. But I don't have to justify myself. I like going out, getting drunk and other things I'm not going to talk about. But everyone wants to be a rocker or in a rap band, so this is something off the wall and different. Maybe we are rebelling against the conformity of being in leather-jacket-wearing rock bands.' The speaker could have been Michael himself. The idea that by returning to older musical standards they were somehow reacting against the grunge rock generation was an appealing one and it also explained, if so many in their age group were doing the same, just why they had so many fans.

And, of course, the two of them were not alone. The new jazz/swing/call-it-what-you-will movement was now in full swing (as it were) and women were involved, too. Amy Winehouse was beginning to take the world by storm, and Katie Melua was also making waves. Exactly the same charges were levelled at her: that there was something strange about harking back to the tastes of an earlier generation and that her music was a little bland. This did not go down well.

'I'm so unconservative,' she retorted to one interviewer who had suggested the opposite. 'That's so funny. Also, I don't think that my music is conservative because of the climate it's in. If everyone else was doing jazzy bluesy folky things in the charts, then you could accuse me of being conservative. But everyone's doing R&B and hip hop and it's the same old tune and the same old video and this is completely different. So how can that be conservative?' How indeed?

Like Michael, Jamie could blow very hot and cold about how he liked to be categorised. One minute he was a jazz singer; the next he was something else. And Jamie didn't like the 'throwback to the fifties' label either. When his album *Catching Tales* was released in 2005, he pointed out that he'd written or co-written most of the tracks himself, something he hoped would stop him being labelled a jazz singer. He went on to add, 'I'm always grouped with Katie Melua, who is a really sweet girl, and Michael Bublé, who is a flawless singer, but I'm not sure where I fit in to all that. My approach is a bit more poppy.'

Nonetheless, this new group of singers had clearly introduced a new type of music to the teen market, one that was totally different from what had gone before. That was apparent everywhere you looked: for example, in 2005, plans were announced to open a new venue in Edinburgh, dedicated to jazz. The old BBC building on Queen Street was to turn into The Jam House. The project was backed by Jools Holland, who had been playing this sort of music before the current crowd of exponents had even been born; even so, set up as an alternative to London's Ronnie Scott's, it was clearly inspired by the new crowd.

'There are a lot of young people who are now becoming interested in jazz music – jazz fans aren't all old people,' said Tom Ponton, a city councillor and member of the Jazz and Blues Festival board. 'People underestimate the interest – Edinburgh has some excellent school jazz bands and jazz has always been encouraged in the city's schools. But it's down to the likes of Jamie Cullum and Michael Bublé that young people are now seeing them as pop stars in their own right, and they are introducing a whole new generation to this style of music.' Whatever Michael and Jamie might have felt about that, he was undeniably right.

Despite his unofficial role as godfather to this new breed of emerging musicians, however, Michael Parkinson himself felt that he no longer had the scope to introduce new talent that he had formerly enjoyed in his heyday in the 1970s. Whereas once he could have given a whole show to a fairly unknown jazz musician, these days the most coverage they could receive, helpful as it was, was a couple of singing slots. Although he was named in 2007 by Q magazine as one of the most influential people currently working on the music scene, television bosses no longer allowed him to feature jazz in the way they once had done. Television had changed, demanding constant variety and a plethora of big-name stars. It would be impossible, these days, to devote a whole show to just one person, especially if there were concerns that that person wasn't very well known. And there was something in this: while Michael had had his British break appearing on *Parkinson*, it was impossible to imagine him getting a whole show to himself. Indeed, even the biggest names of the day were not accorded that. Television audiences' attention span was shorter than ever and they needed constant novelty to keep them tuning in.

Parky certainly missed the good old days, which, incidentally, were at around the time when Michael and Jamie were born. 'We did a seventy-to-eighty-minute show with Duke Ellington, which the BBC put out in its entirety,' he reminisced to Helen Mayhew on *My Jazz*, which was broadcast on the digital radio station The Jazz. 'Can you see that happening now? They'd say Duke who? Not just the BBC but ITV, any of them. "Duke who? Can you get David Beckham on with him? Charlotte Church singing, maybe?" Ah, the decline of British television. In the seventies when I first started, I would have on – as regular guests – Oscar [Peterson], Woody Herman, Buddy Rich. Duke Ellington was there. All were acceptable in those days. No one would raise an eyebrow and say why are you not having the top of the pops on? Nowadays if you suggest somebody like that, they say, "Ooh

I don't know . . . who? What's he done?" It's sad. There's a generation of people running broadcasting, running television particularly, nowadays who have no musical culture beyond that which exists in the top ten.'

What was also sad, for up-and-coming young singers, at least, was that Parkinson announced that he was to retire at the end of the series then going out in 2007 – his last show was in November of that year. The great champion of all these singers had finally had enough.

For some writers, most notably those young male rock critics who so loathed the new musical trend and blamed the veteran television presenter for a lot of it, Parky's disappearance from the scene couldn't come soon enough. 'Listening to Parkinson's musical guests is like being ever so slowly drowned in warmed-over, cloyingly perfumed yak butter,' wrote Rob Fitzpatrick in the *Guardian*. But although fellow angry young men might have agreed with him, the majority did not. Parky was catering for what the public wanted: they did not go out to buy simply because he was telling them to. The music scene had changed, whether the angry young man brigade wanted it to or not. The likes of Michael – a young man, as so many others of the new swingers (in musical terms) were also young – were capturing the popular imagination, giving new form to a music that was vibrant, appealing and catchy and had stood the test of time.

None other than Nancy Sinatra certainly thought so, finding it particularly moving that a new generation of stars was keeping her father's flame glowing. 'It keeps those brilliant songwriters alive, the Cole Porters and Irving Berlins,' she said. 'They live again through people like Jamie Cullum, Michael Bublé and Harry Connick Jr.' (Then again, it must be said that, given the sensitivity the new singers displayed at being compared to the old greats, perhaps Nancy's contribution was not appreciated as much as it otherwise might have been.)

But it really was Parky himself who was the ultimate champion of all this, and after he stepped down from his final show he voiced his regret that no one stepped into his shoes. 'I think it's really sad,' he said. 'BBC Radio 2 should be the natural home of this music; there's a market out there that feels starved of it. What really annoys me is when you see something like *The X Factor* and they say, "She's got a voice like Billie Holiday." Come here, I want to punch you! You never listened to Billie Holiday in your life!' The extent of his love affair with the music was revealed in September 2008: Parky announced he would be releasing a new record in November, *My Life In Music*, a compilation featuring his favourite artists. Michael was there, along with Frank Sinatra, Nat King Cole and Elton John.

And Michael and the rest were probably correct in understanding that the old songs offered a certainty that just wasn't there any more. People needed some assurance that life was not all bad. With the melodies, the subject matter, the sheer lyricism of what all these young crooners were doing, people got, if not certainty, at last something reassuring, familiar, popular and, well, good.

Of course, it was a little irritating for the new crooners to have to hear themselves lumped into one box. But it didn't matter. Ultimately, no matter how annoying it was for these talented young men and women to bear interminable comparisons with each other and the past, the reason for their success is irrelevant. They have won. The angry young rock critics have not had it their way; nor for that matter the naysayers they had all experienced in the past. Not all of this new generation of talent had, like Michael, to put up with borderline bullying at school, but they had all had plenty of detractors on the way up and now they were at the top.

And of course, there was one last element that might have helped them: one Michael himself has been aware of. It is that we live in a post-9/11 world. It is not stretching it too far to say that people, young and old, need security in a way they never have done before and it is perhaps for that reason that they seek out music with charm and reassurance, that talks about everyday hopes and dreams. As Michael himself surmised, that music was warm and comforting in dark times, and people were aware of the need to preserve it now that the greats of yesteryear had all gone. 'We lost Sinatra, we lost Dean Martin, Al Martino,' he said sombrely. 'All the great old singers have gone now, and people miss them. The world has got a lot scarier in the past ten years, and I think people are on a search for something to take them away from that.' Kurt Cobain, Nirvana's lead singer, killed himself, after all, and that, along with his music, does not calm a population desperate to rediscover some certainties, some reassurance that not everything in life is bad.

The suicidal lyrics of the likes of Cobain were in many ways an indulgence for an affluent and prosperous nation when times were good: a way of engaging with the dark side while living an extremely comfortable life. After 9/11, and again, a few years later, when economic catastrophe struck, people didn't want to engage with the dark side any more. They were all too aware it was there: some of them were right smack in the middle of it. Listening to Michael singing 'Mack the Knife' was a way of forgetting about it, putting their troubles behind them and buckling down, instead, to a bit of fun.

These young men and women, above all Michael, with his

smooth stage manner, his earthy sense of humour, his confession to Parkinson that he went into music in order 'to get laid', provided an antidote to growing worldwide angst. And if it brought up visions of Sinatra swaggering through Las Vegas in the glory days, so what? Sinatra didn't become one of the greatest entertainers of the twentieth century without having something to offer: that voice and those songs charmed a world racked by the Second World War, the Cuban missile crisis, the Cold War, Vietnam and any amount of other turbulence as well. If the heirs to his throne have taken on not just the mantle of the songs, but that of the entertainment that somehow blots out the fear and melancholy that so many feel about so much in the world today, then they deserve even more success than they have already had. Michael, Jamie et al. don't just sing about universal issues: they remind us we're all in it together and that fundamentally we all have the same hopes and dreams. It's hardly any wonder that they have carried the world before them and performed with such staggering success.

7

It's Time

By 2005, after a relatively short time at the top of the music scene, Michael really was experiencing the kind of life he could formerly only have dreamt about. Sell-out shows at the Sydney Opera House, the Royal Variety Performance in front of Prince Charles, and now, over three million in worldwide sales. He had become stratospherically successful, but one of the elements that meant most to him was when he was able to take Mitch on tour to Italy with him. It was Grandpa's home country, and now Sunshine had made it big there, too.

'I was able to bring him to Italy with me for concerts where his family is from and his roots are based,' said a clearly emotional Michael. 'He would ask me, after my first record came out, "Are you famous in Italy yet? Is anything happening in Italy yet?" When we hit in Italy, we hit big and he couldn't get over it. We got off the plane and he turned into a fourteen-year-old.'

He did more than that: he turned into a stage performer, too. Michael was not letting this tour go on without his grandfather experiencing something of the euphoria of facing an audience, and so every night he got Mitch to come on stage and say hello in Italian. The crowds loved it and so did Mitch. 'He was having the time of his life,' said Michael, and so he was. The bond between grandfather and grandson had always been a strong one and it was growing stronger still. Michael hadn't just forged a career on the back of the songs he'd learned for his grandpa: now he was actually taking Grandpa back to the past. When Mitch had left Italy all those years ago, he could not possibly have expected to see those shores again, let alone in the company of a grandson who had become a household name. It was a highly emotional experience for them both; it was hard to say which of them felt more moved.

Mitch's presence was good for Michael in other ways, too. It can be a lonely experience going out on the road, one of the reasons so many performers fall prey to drink and drugs. Michael, however, had apparently managed to avoid temptation, and one of the reasons was that he had his grandpa to talk to, although even Grandpa was taken aback at quite how relentless it all was. 'The schedule is just too tough,' he said. 'He's a hard-working kid. I can't believe how hard.' But there was no sign of dangerous excess. 'I'm bragging again, but this kid hasn't changed from day one,' Grandpa Mitch said.

Michael himself, understandably, laughed off suggestions that he was working too hard. He'd seen how his father and grandfather had worked, and while touring might have been hectic, there was no comparison with the life the older generations in his family had led. They didn't get to stay in five-star hotels, cocooned from reality, being chauffeured in private cars and private jets all over the world, and he hadn't forgotten that. There are plenty of performers who have all that and still whine about what they have to do to stay on top. Michael was not about to fall into that trap. Those months he had spent on the boat with his father hadn't been all that long ago.

And then there was Grandpa Mitch himself. 'He's one to talk, working too damn hard,' said Michael of Mitch's remarks. 'You know that house we were in? He built that with his bare hands. Listen, I'm not working half as hard as he did or my father does.'

But there was a downside to his new life, too, and having Grandpa Mitch on side made it considerably easier to cope with. The fact that Michael was singing so many of the songs made famous by the greats meant that he was frequently compared to those greats, and not always favourably. Some critics went so far as to compare him to a hyped-up karaoke singer – surely a ludicrous view, even for those who didn't warm to the Bublé charm – and Michael was having to learn to be tough to survive. This was made easier by the fact that he had some pretty prestigious admirers, too.

'Just last night a fellow named Tom Dreesen, who worked with Sinatra for seventeen years, said to me that I was the only one who was going to be capable of keeping the torch going,' Michael rather defiantly told one interviewer. 'Not only that, I just watched Tony Bennett on television and the interviewer said, "Tony, of all these young kids coming up do you have a favourite?" He said, "No, I can't say that I do," then he stopped and said, "Well, yes, I do actually, it's Michael Bublé." He said he hadn't seen "anything like it since the young Sinatra" and he said, "He can sing anything and make it his own, and I'm a huge fan." A million critics can say I suck, but to hear Tony Bennett say that, I know I'm doing the right thing.'

It was reassuring, but there was also something star-struck about that remark. Michael might have been moving among the biggest names on the planet as their equal for a while now, but there was still something about him of the small-town boy from Canada who couldn't quite believe he'd actually made it. Tony Bennett – the Tony Bennett? To receive an endorsement from one of the names he'd idolised when he himself was growing up was awesome. No wonder that he was able to shrug off the critics: with admirers like that, who needed anyone else? And even more, Michael had broken Italy, which Tony Bennett himself never had. Not only was he keeping the music alive, but he was doing so in countries – his country – that had never heard it the first time around. What singer, what entertainer, wouldn't have been swept away by that?

Unsurprisingly, it was a thrilling moment for Michael when the duo actually met. 'People like Tony Bennett are idols of mine,' he confessed to one interviewer, again showing that star-struck side. 'He is the coolest dude. He is one of the few men I have idolised who haven't disappointed me when I finally met them. I was in Italy last year in a hotel room and he called me and said, "We're staying in the same hotel. Come down for dinner." I went down and he said, "Michael, I'm so proud of you keeping this music alive. I am so excited to see that the young people in Italy are getting it because the record company never broke me back here." I am very proud to say that he is my friend and my mentor.' It must also have meant the world to Grandpa Mitch.

And there were plenty of critics to stick up for him, too. Liz Smith, one of the biggest names in American journalism, was a fan: 'Sings and swings as a sexy, modern version of Frank,

Dino and Sammy,' she said. In Britain, the *Sunday Times* was equally praising: 'He croons like Sinatra and drives women wild,' it said. Complimentary as all this was, it could get a little wearisome. At times, Michael longed for the comparisons, flattering as they were, to stop and for fans and critics alike to start judging him as himself, rather than as a link to an earlier age.

He retained a strongly self-deprecating side as well. Those many years of slogging around before he made it stood Michael in good stead, for he still failed to take himself too seriously, often remarking that his record label treated him like a monkey. 'They feed me pellets and I do the show,' he said on the phone to one writer. 'When I hang up from you, they'll come and take the monkey, put him on to an airplane and fly him to Paris. I like wearing the nice suits, but they put a little hole in the bum so my tail can stick out.' It was an endearing turn of phrase.

And Michael was well aware how strange his life had become. 'I live in a fantasy world,' he said, adding that he was now getting his family to tour with him, in the States, at least. 'Nonetheless, I think I can enjoy it if I keep in mind that it's not real life. Onstage you have to be one person, bigger than life, and it's important to turn that off when you get off-stage. Be a quiet guy who loves his family. You can stick the monkey on the road for two years, but if you put the monkey's family with him he'll just keep going. Listen to me: the monkey likes it!'

But now it was time to return to the studio. For all his success, Michael had not been tested a second time: there was still just a small chance that this might all have been a fluke. And this time round, of course, there was a heavy weight on Michael's shoulders. Previously, he'd had nothing to prove: if the first album hadn't worked, David Foster and Warner Bros wouldn't have been very pleased, but since no one had heard of him, he'd have been able to back off, pride intact, and do something quite new. This time round everyone had heard of him. If he made a mess of it now, the whole world was going to know. Michael was aware of that, too.

'I'm still at that stage where I don't want it to go away,' he explained. 'Fear of failure drives me.' Referring to a journalist who said he had the ability to be one of life's legends, Michael continued, 'It's a beautiful thing that writer said and it makes me feel good when I hear something like that, but I really can't let it get to me. I can't believe it's true. If I do, I have to believe the reviewers who say I'm a piece of crap and scum and I have no business singing. It's weird how melody and harmony added correctly to the right lyrics can touch off an emotional response you really have no power over. It either gives you a burst of energy or you feel the moment or it takes you back.'

He was, however, ensuring that his feet stayed on the ground. The Q magazine debacle was still fresh in everyone's mind. Lesson learned, Michael was not risking anything along those lines again. He might have had the success he'd always dreamed of, but he finally had properly worked out what was really important in life. 'I look at my dad and grandpa and I hope I can be half as successful as they are,' he said. 'They are regular blue-collar guys whose families love them to death. They are loved unconditionally by me and their relatives. One day this may all go away. If it does, I have what's important.'

At other times, Michael would make remarks that would almost unwittingly betray how far he'd come. There was no side to him, as when he earnestly related the story of one night he'd been playing in LA and Chris Isaak, Paul Anka and David Foster joined him on stage: 'I think the people in the audience were beside themselves, because they just didn't expect to see that kind of star power.' They might not have done, but Michael himself was fast reaching the giddy heights now graced by the three other men.

This time round, too, Michael was to have a little more say in what he was about to do. Having been entirely led by the record company when making his first album, by now he'd earned the right to have greater input. He wasn't being foolish, though, and neither was anyone involved in the project. There was to be his first self-penned number, 'Home', but most of the record was to be taken up with the greats of yesteryear.

'It's taking my love of standards and adding it to David Foster's pop sensibility,' Michael explained to one interviewer. 'It's almost making a hybrid that doesn't end up in jazz or sitting in pop. That's why I wrote "Home", so I could cross over to that audience that hadn't been exposed to what I'm doing. When you're working with standards, you don't have to worry about whether there will be any filler on your album. I have to go to the record store and buy too many records for fourteen to fifteen bucks and I only wanted a song or two. What I love so much about standards is you've got thirteen out of thirteen songs you want.'

David Foster was bubbling over with enthusiasm for this latest winner in his showbiz stable. 'It's like working with Beethoven,' he said, becoming only ever so slightly hyperbolic about his young find. 'The man simply is the greatest. People give him flak and reviewers are tough on him, but there is just no denying this man is incredible. He hears things before they happen, like a good athlete.' It was high praise indeed.

In actual fact, however, there had been more discussion behind the scenes about the direction of the new record than everyone at times let on. Having produced such a smash the first time round, David Foster was inclined to play it safe, and release exactly the same kind of offering again: it was Michael who, for all his various reasons, wanted to do something a little different. And this time he won through. It took a certain amount of guts. Michael was becoming established – but he wasn't yet that established. There was still plenty of time for it all to go very badly wrong.

David Foster, however, respected the guts shown by his young protégé. Michael was making a stand for himself now, and plenty of people wouldn't have done. But at the same time, he knew when to shut up. 'He's said it a hundred times,' said Michael. '"I'd make the same record. I'd make a safe record." But when we finished the record, he actually called me. He said, "I'm really proud of you," because he said, "You interfered just enough." He said, "You pushed your weight around, but when it needed to happen, you let me do my job." I know that David cares about me, and I'm very close to him and everything. But listen, if my second CD goes to . . . he just goes on and produces his next artist. It's over. So there's a lot on the line for me. So I really wanted it to be great.'

The name of the new album came about after some deliberation, as Michael took a certain glee in explaining. 'The truth is, I wanted to call the record *Feeling Good*,' he said. 'And I think a lot of people at the label thought it sounded a lot like country music. "And ahmmm fee-lin' gooood!" I (eventually) said, "Listen, you can call it 'It's Crap' if you like." I figured if the title of this record has anything to do with my success or my failure, you know, I'm in the wrong business.'

When Michael's first album came out, he was beside himself with joy: now, however, he was beginning to express doubts that might well have surfaced only after some pretty severe knocks. Although he claimed to be impervious to criticism, some of it must have hurt and Michael did occasionally sound slightly defensive, whether he realised it or not. One of the biggest gripes against him – the criticism that he didn't sing many original songs (this was to be corrected on the second album) – might, over time, have affected his attitude to that first album. 'The second record I knew had to be better than the first,' he said. 'I knew I had to like it more. I became less and less impressed with myself. More than less impressed, I became disappointed in what I had done. Not that it was terrible, or that I had ripped someone off, I just thought I could have sung this record so much better.'

This was a telling remark. A few years previously, it wouldn't have occurred to Michael that he was ripping anyone off, or indeed even occurred to him to have used that phrase. But it was what he'd heard a lot of over the previous few years from his detractors, and it had clearly hit home. Not that he conceded they had a point (they didn't), but that he was used to having to deal with accusations from all sides now. This was almost a way of pre-empting the criticism before it came. Indeed, on another occasion he admitted, 'It sucks when the critics don't like you. I don't care who you are and what artists say, but you do care when critics don't like you.' He certainly did.

But he did, like other singers with real staying power, have the ability not only to rise above it, but to realise that ultimately, however much the critics' barbs stung, his audience was the most important thing. The critics might like or hate him, but it was the people who bought his records that mattered most. In that, he could have looked to another star, one of the few to whom he hadn't been compared, but a major mainstream singing star who had lasted for decades now, and that was Barry Manilow. Manilow was another one who was constantly patronised by angry young men and cool rock critics: given that he had managed by now, however, to fashion a career that had lasted for decades, it is safe to say that that cannot have weighed too heavily on his mind. It must be said that Manilow and Michael were not like and like. But Manilow, as much as any star in the last century, realised that the connection with his fans was crucial, and that he must give them what they wanted. Michael, in a very different way, was cottoning on to that, too. Do the new record as he wanted it to be done, be prepared to experiment a little – but be aware of what it was that the fans wanted next. Surprise them, enchant them, but don't let them down.

It was a balancing act that Michael was to bring off to brilliant effect. 'I had to wake up one morning and make a conscious decision,' he said. 'I'm going to make this record for the people, not for the critics.' In the event, the critics loved it – much to his relief, as Michael would have been the first to admit – but this was a clear sign that he realised it was his fans, not the music press, who were to be the most important people on the road that lay ahead.

There were other elements at play, as well. Rather than simply mimicking the singers he loved, as he had done in the early days, Michael felt his voice had finally come into its own. 'Now I think I've found myself, and I have such joy for what I do that whatever naturally comes out, comes out. I love what I do, and I believe in what I'm doing. I hope I'm confident without being a real egotistical jerk, you know? But I definitely feel confident and excited about every night.'

Rather surprisingly, and bravely, he was also thinking about covering some of his contemporaries' music. 'Chris Martin of Coldplay,' he said. 'I think Maroon 5 is great. There's a Canadian named Ron Sexsmith, who's turned out to be a good friend. Bryan Adams and Jim Vallance had a big impact on me. I'm also a huge fan of Oasis.'

There were other changes from his first outing, too, not least the decision to ask Nelly Furtado to work on the new album. The two duetted on 'Quando, Quando, Quando'. 'I wanted someone young, I wanted someone who sings beautifully, and I wanted someone who sells records internationally and can speak Portuguese,' he said. 'So I'm thinking, "Yeah, there are people like that everywhere." And all of a sudden, I thought, Nelly Furtado!'

She had not, in fact, been the first choice. That honour had gone to Renee Olstead, but suddenly everyone woke up to the fact that she was little more than a child, and that might cause raised eyebrows in some quarters. Michael was certainly aware of that particular danger. 'I had to call her and say, "Honey, I'm your biggest fan but I can't sing this song to you,"' he explained. 'I said, "You need to understand you killed it. It's just that you're fifteen and I'm twenty-nine years old. I can't look at you and go, 'When will you be mine? Quando, quando, quando . . . child molester.'"'

Michael might have put his bad-boy ways behind him, but he could be a bit of a handful, all the same. Interviewed once in Nelly's presence, Michael told her of her singing 'I'm Like a Bird', 'I thought you were really cute, Nelly. Your eyes. I wanted to pop them out and keep them. Nelly, if you were a Popsicle, know what I'd do with you? I'd take off your wrapper and hold you by your two little sticks and I would lick you up the centre and then I would break you in half on the

counter and put half of you in the freezer for later.'
Fortunately, Debbie was present: 'Only Michael can get away
with stuff like that,' she said.

The weight of expectation might have been a lot heavier
than it once was, but Michael was a lot more mainstream
than he'd been when he started out, too. That was due in part
to his own success – when you've sold three million records,
you can no longer be called niche music – but also because
popular tastes were continuing to change. The kind of music
Michael made was becoming popular in itself again. Even so,
things had changed. The first time round, with his major
debut album, it was only David Foster's balls that were on the
line (in Michael's words). Now his own were there, too.

But he was giving it everything he'd got. Unsurprisingly, he
was bullish about the new work. 'I think *It's Time* is much
better than anything I've done before,' he declared in one
interview. 'I've always written a lot of my own songs, but
didn't get the chance to put any on my debut album. This
time I've been able to include one called "Home" and I'm
really proud as everyone thinks it will be the hit. The other
songs are a mix of all-time classics including Stevie Wonder's
"You and I", featuring Stevie himself on harmonica.' Again,
that last, almost throwaway comment was a sign of just how
far he'd come. Other songs included 'Feeling Good', 'A
Foggy Day (In London Town)', 'Can't Buy Me Love' and
'How Sweet It Is'. He also sang 'The More I See You' and
'Song For You'.

Michael saw the new album as a development in many
directions. 'I was a purist,' he said. 'Now, I get a great kick out
of taking David Foster's and [fellow producer] Humberto
Gatica's pop sensibility and blending it with my purist taste. I
wanted my album to sound like Bennett and Sinatra, but

when I take these two styles, it creates a hybrid that's much more powerful for the listener who isn't a purist; for the young kid in America, the thirteen-year-old, who doesn't get the big-band sound.'

Another reason for Michael to feel pleased about the inclusion of 'Home' was that, given that he'd written it himself, he would be paid far more than if he'd sung someone else's song, as he would get a publishing royalty. It also set down a marker for a potential career to come. If Michael were able to develop in such a way that he not only penned his own music, but that of other people as well, the sky was his limit to an even greater extent than the opportunities before him now.

The choice of music also reflected the amount of touring Michael had done. He knew what his audiences liked: he knew what worked. His increased experience allowed him to judge the mix within the music, and he knew it, too. 'I want to be tangible to my audience,' he said. 'I've performed in everything from small clubs to major concert halls. It's been a tremendous confidence builder, which I think is reflected in the performances on my new album, and it gave me a chance to try out some of the new material and find out what worked. I think the sessions really benefited from having come straight off the road into the studio. Between David, Humberto Gatica and I, we were fanatical about getting just the right balance of songs to put on the record. There may be better pop singers and jazz singers out there, but nobody has as much passion for this music as I do and I think you can hear that on the record.'

The release of this record, however, was so different from that of the previous one that he still couldn't believe quite how far he'd come and how fast. 'I felt it starting to move,' he said wonderingly. 'You feel the energy around you, you see records selling and you go from playing a 200-seat club to being in a 4,000- or 10,000-seat theatre. I knew there was pressure on me to come out with a record that was better than the first. I was nervous for about a year and a half, but I did a lot of homework so when I went into the studio I was really ready.'

To coincide with the release of the album, Ian 'Molly' Meldrum, the foremost television pop critic in Australia, flew to Vancouver to make a film about the boy wonder. 'He's opened up a whole new audience to those songs,' Meldrum explained. Michael, meanwhile, recited the list of countries he'd been touring since the release of the first album: 'If you can imagine, I never left North America until a few years ago – these are places I saw in movies,' he explained. 'It blows my mind that you've flown from Australia to my home town to talk to me.' Meldrum was even filming the family boat, *Winning Edge*: Lewis and Amber, while not quite the subject of such curiosity as their famous son, were sought-after inter-viewees, too. There was also a great deal of curiosity about Michael's sisters, about his personal life – about everything to do with him. It was heady stuff.

Another appearance on Michael Parkinson's show beck-oned. Michael was looking forward to that, too. 'I met Sean Connery on the Michael Parkinson show,' he explained. 'I was wearing a Chelsea jersey because I support them and like to watch them at Stamford Bridge whenever I am in London. Sir Sean came up to me afterwards and said, "Michael. I like your music, but you should be wearing a Rangers jersey." So I said, "OK, Sean. Next time. I promise." I was a bit intimi-dated. What a cool dude he is though.' He really had made it: advice from James Bond. And not only that: he was showing an interest in football, despite the fact that Canadians, Michael among them, were so famously addicted to hockey. How could he fail to win Britain round?

Nor had he forgotten what the first appearance had done for his career. 'Michael Parkinson has been wonderful for me,' Michael continued. 'Not only has he been a great and generous man, but he is brilliant at what he does. I went on his show for the first time and I was blown away. His skills as an entertainer and interviewer are second to none. I wish we had someone like that in America. When I saw his Meg Ryan interview, I wanted to hit her. He was a class act and she was a bitch.' Again, Michael was displaying the trait that helped his career no end: utter empathy with his audience. He defended Parkinson against Meg Ryan, a fellow North American. Heck, he'd even taken the trouble to find out about the furore that surrounded Parkinson's toe-curling interview with Ryan (she'd answered his questions in monosyllables and then told him to wrap it up). How could he fail to have a British audience eating out of his hand?

When *It's Time* finally came out on 8 February 2005, it exceeded everyone's expectations. It entered the charts at number one in Canada, Italy, Spain, Japan and Singapore, number five in Britain and, most importantly of all, number seven on the *Billboard* charts in the States, one of few countries that had seemed rather resistant to Michael's winning ways. He was especially pleased about that last. 'I tell you something. [The record chain] Target ordered 30,000 records,' he said gleefully. 'They sold them in one day. They had to give out IOUs. I sold 92,000 copies in America on the first day.' If he sounded a little boastful, who could blame him? Who could criticise those sorts of numbers or query how far he'd come?

It was certainly a relief after what he saw as the relative failure of his first album in the States, which sold a mere 920,000 copies. 'America just didn't get it,' he said. 'Per capita, it's a huge failure. They couldn't get the TV and the things I needed. So I said, "I'm going to go where I'm wanted." I tell you why America is so shocked this week. Because I had no TV appearances [last week]. I did the *Today* show and [David] Letterman this week. That's why they're going, "Holy shit."'

One paradox about the situation in which he now found himself, however, was that in some countries, even those in which his records sold in the millions, Michael was still not recognised in the street. He was smart enough to realise that that could have advantages, though. For one thing, it afforded him a freedom that not many stars of his stature managed to maintain, and for another, it meant that there was still another mountain to climb. Challenges were good. Challenges were for him. 'I love being the underdog,' he said. 'I know a lot of people still don't know who I am, even though I have sold more records than people who are huge, but it suits me.' It was true, though, that he was differentiating more and more between private and public life. Because Michael was still spending a huge amount of time out on the road, there wasn't much time for a private life; it also meant that when he did get time to himself, he appreciated it as never before.

For now, though, the publicity machine was in full swing and so was the promotional one. Michael worked quite as hard as he had done previously: it was, after all, in his own interests to make this album sell as well as it could. 'I did three music videos in about three days,' he said at one stage. 'The next morning after the last video, I got on an airplane and I flew to France, I got there about six o'clock in the morning, Paris time, went to a TV show, did press all day . . .'

His efforts were not in vain. Michael had a spectacular success with the album, and the same again with the single

Strike a pose: Michael plays up to the part. Photographed in 2006.

(Ken McKay/Rex Features)

Family values: Michael's sister Crystal is also in show business – she works as an actress.

(Christopher Morris/Corbis)

Lifting his spirits: Michael and actor Brody Hutzler lend support to actress Maeve Quinian at the premiere of Totally Blonde, 17 December, 2001. (Frederick M Brown/Getty Images)

Baby you can drive my – rickshaw. Manila, 2004.

(CAMERA PRESS/Nick Wilson)

Playing the game: Michael is a massive hockey fan and is pictured here as a Canucks guest radio commentator with sports broadcaster John Shorthouse during the game at General Motors Placeon 7 February, 2009 in British Columbia. (Photo by Jeff Vinnick/NHLI via Getty Images)

Mystery man: But Michael is also a bit of a bloke. Photographed in New York in 2007.
(Matthew Salacuse/Retna)

Make mine a double: Michael tries (and fails) to break the world record for drinking a 500ml milkshake on the Paul O'Grady Show, London 9 November, 2005.
(Ken McKay/Rex Features)

The man and his mentor: Michael talking to Michael Parkinson, the man who was largely responsible for launching his career in the UK, on the Parkinson show, 24 November, 2007

Seeing double: Michael and his producer David Foster before a charity fund raising dinner for the David Foster Foundation in Vancouver in 2006.

American Idol: Tony Bennett and the young pretender (Tony Bennett: An American Classic, 2006). (NBCUPHOTOBANK/Rex Features)

Feted all over the world: Michael appears on the German television show Wetten Dass in Leipzig on 10 November, 2007. (Sven Hoogerhuis/LFI)

Larking about: Michael and his then girlfriend Emily Blunt celebrate her nomination for two Golden Globe Awards in 2006. (Armando Gallo/Retna)

New love: Michael Buble poses with his new girlfriend, Argentinian actress Luisana Lopilato, at the 57th Annual BMI Pop Awards in Beverly Hills, California May 19, 2009.
(REUTERS/Fred Prouser/UNITED STATES ENTERTAINMENT)

Michael might not read Chatelaine, but he is one of the very few men to have appeared on its cover. September, 2008.

The ladies' man: Michael charms his female fans at a performance in *David Foster & Friends*, a tribute to producer David Foster on May 23, 2008 at Mandalay Bay in Las Vegas, Nevada. (Photo by Frank Micelotta/Getty Images)

One for the road: Michael is presented with a gold plaque at his end of tour party at Lugo Caffe in New York on 5 December, 2008. From left to right, Dion Singer, Mitra Darab, Michael Buble, John Esposito, Bruce Allen, Dox Fox, Diarmuid Quinn and Humberto Gatica. (Joe Kohen/WireImage for Warner Brothers Records)

Friends in high places: Michael is pictured with Tanya Kim and Ben Mulroney at the 2009 Juno awards in Vancouver. Ben's father Brian was instrumental in discovering the young star. (George Pimentel/WireImage)

'Home'. The United States was beginning to sit up and take notice; he'd taken on the critics who said he never sang anything original and he'd proved he had another talent: as a songwriter. It was time, indeed.

8

The Devil Wears Bublé

The event: the *TV Week* Logie Awards, held in Australia. The year: 2005. Michael was in Oz shortly before the break-up of his relationship with Debbie to promote his latest record and while doing so attended the event: also there on the evening was a young British actress who was making quite a name for herself. She was called Emily Blunt, and was in town to make the thriller *Irresistible* with Sam Neill and Susan Sarandon. Michael had no idea who she was, however, and thought she worked for the BBC. Anyway, Emily had a boyfriend and Michael had a girlfriend. 'As we shook hands, I thought how cute she was, but I was in my relationship and she was in one, too,' said Michael. And there matters lay.

Except they didn't. A few months later, with both of them now single, Emily went to a Michael Bublé concert in LA, and the two met again. Neither was keen to rush into any-thing, and yet something clearly was there. There had been an attraction at the first meeting and there was an attraction at the second. But both were being cautious. 'I wasn't in great shape mentally, nor was she,' said Michael, some time after the relationship had taken off. 'We'd both come out of long relationships. We took it slowly, became friends first, which is something I've not done too often. And it's been great.'

Michael and Emily were, for a time, to become a golden couple. He was young and handsome, she was young and beautiful; he was a singer, she was an actress; he was established, her star was shooting up – it was a match made in show-business heaven. More than that, however, they seemed made for each other. Both had the same earthy sense of humour, both eschewed the Hollywood party scene, both were down to earth, both came from close-knit families and both, for a while, were crazy about each other. What could possibly go wrong?

Emily Olivia Leah Blunt was born in Roehampton, west London, on 23 February 1983. What she did not have in common with Michael was her social background, given his working-class origins: she came from the comfortable middle class, one of four children of a barrister father and teacher mother. Her uncle, Christopher Blunt, moreover, is a Conservative MP. Emily comes across as very prim and proper: her appearance and her demeanour speak of the Ice Queen, although in reality she is far more down to earth. Right from the word go she seemed set on an acting career. She attended a sixth form college called Hurtwood House, which was known for its performing arts programme; while still at school, she attracted an agent. Emily was on her way.

By the time Michael met her, she was already carving out a very successful career. Her first appearance was in a musical called *Bliss* by Paul Sellar, at the 2000 Edinburgh Festival, while she was still at school. Appearances at the National

Theatre and Chichester Festival Theatre followed, before her first television drama, *Boudica*, in 2003. She also played the role of Catherine Howard in the television two-parter *Henry VIII*.

But it was the following year that she tasted real professional success. Emily appeared in the film *My Summer of Love*, about a teenage lesbian relationship in the Yorkshire countryside: the film was a great success and Emily and her co-star Nathalie Press shared the *Evening Standard* British Film Award for Most Promising Newcomer. After that came the TV drama *Gideon's Daughter*, written by Stephen Poliakoff, in which Emily played the child of a Labour spin doctor, Gideon Warner, memorably brought to the screen by Bill Nighy. And then came the role for which she is still probably best known: Emily Charlton, *Runway* editor Miranda Priestley's assistant in *The Devil Wears Prada*. Despite the fact that Meryl Streep and Anne Hathaway were the acknowledged stars of the film, Emily carried off the role with such aplomb that *Entertainment Weekly* named her as Best Female Scene-Stealer. And that is about where she was when she and Michael got together. A star in the ascendant, on the brink of a great deal more.

Not that the man himself yet had any idea, on that second meeting, who Emily was. He still thought she worked in television. 'I had it in my head that she was a producer for the BBC and so asked what kind of programmes she made,' he said ruefully some time later. 'And I admit that when she replied that, no, she was an actor, I thought, "Right, like every other person waiting on table." So when in time I saw *My Summer of Love*, to say that I was blown away would be an understatement. I was like, "But you're fucking brilliant!" Then came *Gideon's Daughter* and then *The Devil Wears Prada*. After the premiere of that, I remember turning and saying to her, "Kiddo, you stole the entire movie. Your life is never going to be the same again."' Nor was it – either from the perspective of the film or that of her personal life. A new phase had begun.

The two clicked right from the off. From the very beginning of the relationship right up until the end, Michael was to carry on more like a besotted teenager than an increasingly famous singer: it seemed he just couldn't believe he'd ended up with such a class act on his arm. Cool, beautiful, radiant Emily was what any sensible man would wish for – and he'd got her all to himself. It helped that Michael adored her whole family, too. 'I tried to move slowly because we'd both just come through break-ups but the truth is I was pretty much instantly infatuated,' he admitted. 'I mean, forgetting for a moment how beautiful she is, she's got this wonderful personality and . . . Anyway! Because I was very quickly so crazy about Emily it felt like there was a lot riding on how it went when I first met her parents.'

As with so many young couples, Michael was invited round to meet them over dinner. He was, by his own account, a bag of nerves. 'But the door is opened to me by this big, lanky kid, her fifteen-year-old brother, who straight off gave me a hug,' he recalled. 'How's about that for a welcome? Then she has these two beautiful younger sisters. Her dad is just great – he's teaching me cricket. And her mom? We sat down to eat, and talking to me she was so dry, so British and just so fucking great that, had we been standing up, I'd've had to squeeze her. As it was, I thought, "That's it. I'm gonna have to bite your arm!" and so I did, like this.' (He pretended to bite the interviewer's sleeve.) It was quite clear from this, not only that Michael and Emily shared the same sense of humour, but that Michael chimed in with her entire family, too.

Indeed, he seemed to realise this himself. 'The great thing is I can be myself with them, be rude, swear, whatever and they just laugh,' Michael continued. 'My ex's parents are sweet and lovely but also very proper. I had to be on my best behaviour and couldn't always manage it. Emily's just accept me as the person I am and seem to like me for it. It's such a big, big relief.' Meanwhile, his own parents appeared to be as besotted as Michael himself was: 'They're in love, like me.' Indeed, according to Michael, his mother's attitude was this: 'OK, honestly, her favourite thing about me is my girlfriend.'

In an interview towards the end of 2007, Michael sounded like nothing so much as a teenager in love: 'I like her sense of humour and her reserve,' he said. 'I even like the things I don't like. I was pretty much instantly infatuated as soon as I met her.' This could not have been easy reading for Debbie. After all, throughout the time they were together, Michael had taken a very different attitude. At the beginning of his fame, he had refused to go public on whether or not he had a girlfriend. Then there was his very public bad behaviour and even when he had calmed down and the two of them were back together, their reunion was marked by the publication of the Q profile. They may have got engaged, but ultimately the engagement came to nothing, and Debbie hadn't been on the receiving end of anything like as much public acclamation from her ex-boyfriend. In marked contrast to this previous behaviour, however, Michael couldn't shut up about Emily. In his eyes, it appeared he had pretty much met The One.

His family remained enamoured, too. In many ways it must have come as a relief that Michael appeared to be settling down, after all the reports of womanising and that profile in Q magazine. But, although he and Emily were not formally engaged, it looked as if this was a very serious pairing – the

Bublés clearly hoped so. 'I do love your girlfriend so much,' said Amber in an interview she and her son gave together. 'In fact, if he doesn't marry her, I might kill him. But we'd find someone in the family to marry her because we're not letting her go – ever. She's me in many ways. They're perfect together.'

They made a very glamorous couple, Michael the crooner and Emily the glittering actress, but Michael was adamant that underneath it all, they were just like any young couple in love. 'We don't really mix up too much who we are with what we do,' he said. 'I think we forget with each other. She's a great actor but I look at her and think, "God, she's a little goof!" And then I see a film and I think: "Wow, OK, you're that person, too." Both of us have these lives where we are in different countries and cities every day, but really it's the same as any relationship – it takes time, and a lot of effort and communication. I don't think we are into the Hollywood lifestyle. It's not about avoiding it – it's because we have more fun chilling out at home and playing Nintendo Wii, kicking each other's butts bowling.'

That 'little goof' remark was at the heart of the relationship (in the past, Debbie had referred to Michael's goofiness, too). The two of them were simply sensible enough not to believe their own publicity, on top of which they shared an earthy sense of humour. Both were in the position of being publicly fêted, glamorous beings with enormous fan bases; both felt themselves to be fairly ordinary people underneath. Both understood the pressures of fame; both were glad to be with someone who understood that beneath the superstar image, there was a normal person fighting to get out.

But there was the glitzy side of things, too. He escorted her to the Golden Globe awards, where she won Best Supporting

Actress for *Gideon's Daughter*, and Michael's reaction could not have been more positive if he'd tried; Emily's success made him even happier than did his own. 'That was the greatest night of my career,' he said. 'For one day I got to feel like my family gets to feel. I understand what my mom and dad and grandparents say when they tell me they get more joy out of seeing me succeed than I do.' That sheer generosity of spirit, the joy in another's success and happiness, the abnegation of self – that comes pretty close to fundamental proof of a relationship that really works. It made the ultimate ending all the more sad.

As the relationship developed and became more serious, they began living together, dividing their time between Vancouver and London. 'Which isn't ideal, obviously, but we just do our best with the geography of the situation and are together whenever we can be,' Michael said. But it was an indication of what eventually could go wrong. Both had careers that took them all over the world, which meant that spending quality time together was far more difficult than it would have been in normal circumstances. This was, if anything, more important to Emily than Michael, for she was at a different stage in her career. By the time they met, Michael had well and truly made it, but Emily was in the process of moving from budding starlet to the real deal.

It was *The Devil Wears Prada* that truly pushed her into the spotlight, making it plain that she had the potential to be a very big name in the movies. But it meant that she was often away for her work, as was Michael, and the two of them had to spend a good deal of time apart. Indeed, in the last months of their relationship, there was comment if either attended an awards ceremony or a glittering event without the other. This was frequently down to nothing more ominous than that they had separate work commitments. But it did mean the relationship was under constant external scrutiny, which was bound to put it under strain.

But Michael wanted it to work, whatever the external pressures on the couple might be. It seemed to be important to him that the duo came across as utterly normal, too. 'Neither of us is into the celebrity lifestyle,' he declared. 'We don't have celebrity friends and we don't go to celebrity parties. I'm just a normal guy.' He'd had a few years of it now: he'd worked out who he was, what he wanted and what was important to him. And that most certainly was Emily.

This normal-guy aspect of his personality was a help to Emily, too. Her star was very much on the rise, but as her fame grew, so did the pressures she had to deal with. Michael helped her to cope with a situation she had never experienced before. 'I remember at the New York premiere of *Prada*, the limo pulled up and I was sweating and panicking, and Michael gave me great advice,' she recalled. 'He said, "Calm down, and become someone else, someone who's good at doing the red carpet. Now, get out of the fucking limo!"' Of course, that was exactly what he'd been having to learn himself.

At this stage, Michael still sounded like nothing so much as a besotted teenager. 'Our families match as much as we do,' he told one interviewer, sounding positively gloopy. The international divide between the UK and Canada was proving no problem between himself and Emily and that went for their families, too. 'There's a lot of love going on between them all,' he went on. 'They're all loud and opinionated. Our parents love each other and even get drunk together. My dad had a cigarette at a party and almost burned down my apartment. He blamed Emily's dad and Emily's dad blamed him. There's great banter between them.' Michael and Emily got on; their families got on. Was it any wonder the union seemed bound to be a success?

Michael was adamant that his relationship with Emily even dictated the way he came across on stage. 'There's a big difference in singing a love song when you're in love compared to when you're not. You're not acting, you mean every word,' he said. 'I wrote so many songs when I met Emily because I was happy, inspired and in love. Emily comes with me when I'm on the road. Neither of us want to be defined by our jobs.' Except that sometimes she couldn't come out with him, and while neither wanted to be defined by their jobs, they still wanted those jobs to exist. External pressures were still to take their toll.

But not yet. Emily was even bringing out a romantic side to Michael, one that hadn't been too much evident, in public at least, in the past. 'I'm a romantic but in the small ways,' he said happily. 'I'm not as smooth as I'd like to be or as people think but I'm thoughtful. Emily was making a movie and I had to go on tour. She was crushed about not seeing me for three weeks, so I bought her some nice sheets, flowers, candles and a massage chair and I went into her trailer and decorated it. I wrote notes and hid them everywhere. I put one in the kitchen drawer with a note saying, "When you eat, think about biting me." But I'm not James Bond romantic, I'm more like a bumbling Hugh Grant.'

It was certainly different from the laddish persona he had presented in the past. More than that, reading between the lines, it seemed as if Emily was the one with the greater power in the relationship. Although she was happy to talk about her new boyfriend, it was Michael, not Emily, who seemed besotted: a small-town boy with real Hollywood glamour on his arm.

Emily's Englishness didn't hurt, either: she was a refined lady. Pure class. And beautiful with it, too. She was the epitome of glamour – but still the girl next door. She was as down to earth as Michael. Apart from sharing his earthy sense of humour (his pet name for her was 'Garfield' because of her huge eyes), she, like Michael, felt little need to embrace the celebrity lifestyle. The two of them were very much showing a sense of self and it was to be respected. Both knew who they were: neither appeared to be setting out with anything to prove. Hollywood, Schmollywood. Both knew what was important in life.

'I get it that it's someone else's reality to go out every night and get dressed up,' she told one interviewer. 'But Michael and I don't live that sort of life. We try to maintain a life that's true to us. You might catch me in heels and a nice top on the rare night out. We live in Vancouver, but I spend a lot of my life in hotels, so when I get home I crave nothing more than to cook.'

According to Michael, too, the two really did manage to have a relatively normal lifestyle, with no vast entourages of domestic staff. 'No matter what I'm doing I try to hang out with Emily as much as I can,' said Michael. 'We usually like to cook a lot and watch movies and stuff like that and have a bottle of wine and chat. I think Emily is a better cook. I think it's pretty close though, she's far more inventive. She sometimes reminds me of the rat from *Ratatouille* . . . maybe it's the way she squeaks.'

Emily was also aware that the relationship was provoking a great deal of curiosity. 'Everyone seems so intrigued by it,' she said. 'But we're just us. We really love each other a huge amount. And we both have to work so hard to see each other often. I flew to Australia to spend time with him on tour; he'll fly to sets to be with me. But it's all totally worth it. I loved having him at my side at the Golden Globes last year, my first big American awards show outing. He just makes fun of it, and we had a laugh on the way there. He's probably better at dealing with those situations than I am. He appears highly sophisticated on stage, but I'm telling you, he's not that person. We take a lot with a pinch of salt.' That was the secret to it all: both seemed beyond glamorous and both saw themselves as normal people with an extraordinary lifestyle. It was a very fortuitous match.

Emily was a pretty good sport about having a superstar boyfriend, too, and all the attention he got from other women, recalling one occasion when she was accompanying him on tour. 'About a hundred girls just started running after Michael,' she said. 'I dropped something and bent down to pick it up only to then be bodyslammed against the tour bus by people trying to get to him. The tour manager saw me, grabbed me and yanked me up the stairs of the bus to safety. That was scary.' But she was relieved that of the two of them, her boyfriend was the bigger star. 'It's harder when you're the one emasculating your boyfriend,' she continued. 'It doesn't work. If someone is not fulfilled in what they do and you're a successful girl – it works against you.' She was too right there. Emily was a star – but Michael was even more so. And she had the sense to realise that the balance of power, such as it was, seemed about right.

The two continued to burble about one another. 'Sometimes I even get tears in my eyes when I see him onstage,' said Emily. 'It's overwhelming.' Michael got all choked up, too. 'Every time I see her onscreen, I fall in love with her all over again,' he gushed. But each had to share the other with the public, and with their conflicting career demands. Much as they wanted it to be, their relationship could not be as straightforward as a normal young couple's, because they were not a normal young couple. They worked in the rarified world of show business, and one day, something was going to have to give.

For now, though, there was still a strong bond between them. Emily remained keen to emphasise that Michael was not really the sophisticate so many people saw. 'He's such a geek,' she said. 'We're both a couple of nerds, actually. But I can't elaborate on that. It would be wrong of me to comment on our eccentricities. The women at his gigs love him, anyway. They all throw panties at him.' They might well, however, have been throwing panties while Michael was singing the song he wrote for Emily, 'Everything'. Their future happiness together seemed guaranteed.

She was having an impact on him musically in other ways, too. It is because of Emily that 'Me and Mrs Jones' was included on Michael's third album, initially much to his chagrin. She loved the song; David Foster became convinced that Michael should have it on the album, and so Michael listened to it. Initially, he couldn't believe what he heard. 'I thought it was so cheesy and I just looked at Emily and went, "I can't believe you did this to me,"' was his first reaction. But he changed his mind. 'It's really kind of sexy and hip, and I liked, maybe a little of the cheese in it, you know what I mean?' he continued. Emily was even influencing his music. What could possibly go wrong?

With all this going on, the question seemed to be not if they would get married, but when. Michael seemed to acknowledge as much when he went on a Canadian radio station. 'I really feel like, you know, I'm going to marry her . . . I want to be the dad of her kids,' he announced. 'I haven't proposed to her yet. But I will do that. In a way I'm sort of proposing to her through this interview.'

It was never really clear, perhaps even to Michael himself, whether he'd meant it – that version of a proposal at least. He went on to claim it was a joke that no one understood. 'Do you really think I would pop the question in a fucking gossip magazine?' he demanded of one interviewer. 'I don't think she'd be too thrilled about that.' What if they did get married? Would he sing to Emily at the ceremony? 'Absolutely not,' said Michael firmly. 'No, no, no.' Indeed, he was beginning to sound a little sensitive on the subject of wedding singers, because speculation about his own potential nuptials had reminded everyone of how he made his breakthrough. 'After all those years of not wanting to be a wedding singer, I sing at one fucking wedding, and now I'm the wedding singer who got discovered!' he protested. But did he really care? As long as he and Emily were getting on, all was right with the world.

Several duff notes, however, were beginning to sound. Michael might have been a world-class superstar, but maybe he still felt like the nerdy kid from high school who didn't quite fit in with the rest, and no matter how successful you become, that never truly goes away. And so, while it is entirely possible he wouldn't even admit it to himself, perhaps this was a subconscious testing of the waters. Perhaps he did want to propose to Emily, but was too scared at what the answer might be. And so perhaps he wanted to see what her reaction to this would be, without even realising what he was doing. Emily, of course, on the other hand, might not have appreciated the fact that he was making his intentions clear to the wider world without consulting her first.

Certainly, this marked an abrupt change in the relationship, although in fairness, other factors were in play as well. But alas: it was after this announcement, in November 2007, that trouble in paradise surfaced in a very big way. It seemed that Michael could not escape his past reputation when newspapers were suddenly full of reports of a fling and the media went into a frenzy.

At first, Emily stayed calm, standing beside her boyfriend. After all, she was the openly acknowledged woman in his life. Even though she didn't say so at the time, however – and never has – the embarassment must have been intense. No woman likes public allegations that her boyfriend has been cheating splattered all over the newspapers, even if the allegations are untrue. If that woman is an up-and-coming Hollywood star, so much the worse. It would have been remarkable if the relationship had continued unscathed.

It didn't. Matters went quiet for a while and then started the unmistakable signs that all was not well. Quite how unwell was revealed when Michael made the following declaration: 'We will never be getting married,' he said in June 2008. 'Never. I know I had indicated we would but now it's a total no-no.'

The world was abuzz. What had happened? What had finally caused the split? But when it finally happened, there was merely some talk about the pressures of spending so much time apart. To this day, neither Michael nor Emily has ever said exactly what it was that pushed them apart, but it is hard not to come to the conclusion that the reports of infidelity had something to do with it. Emily Blunt is clearly a proud woman and cannot have enjoyed the media crawling all over her relationship. Michael's frequent and very public protestations of love before it all happened must have made it particularly hard to bear.

After some intensive speculation in the media, the split was finally confirmed by Michael's publicist Liz Rosenberg. 'Sadly, after three years, they have parted ways,' she told the gossip blogger Perez Hilton. 'They are both extraordinary people with huge talent. Let's wish them well.' She wouldn't be drawn any further about what had gone on behind closed doors: everyone was staying resolutely schtumm.

But what a sad outcome to what had once seemed so very positive. And whatever had really been going on, it was Michael who seemed to take the split really badly. Whatever he did, there was no question that he had loved Emily and had seen her as the love of his life. He may not be the first person to learn, too late, that if you have a good relationship it's a very bad idea to allow it to fall apart: great loves do not come along that often in any person's life, even if that person is a world-famous singer. Michael was quite clearly finding it tough.

He made no bones of that fact. 'Emily was a substantial person and amazing still,' he said in an interview with *Entertainment Tonight Canada*, a short time after the split. 'Top girl. Top class.' He didn't sound either as if he'd got over her or as if he'd actually wanted to part.

'In my business it's tough to go out with another artist because you're never together,' Michael said. 'You're lucky if you can see the person once every two to three months, and with Em, she was on her movies and I was doing my thing so it made it more difficult.' Admittedly, Emily's star had risen massively since she and Michael first got together; she was routinely photographed either with or without him at major show business events and was now playing increasingly high profile roles in her films, but still. This was not what they'd said at the beginning. What had happened to her accompanying Michael on tour and his turning up on

Emily's film sets? It was a marked contrast to how they'd started out. And even if her star had grown – she was not exactly without profile – the two of them still seemed a pretty perfect match.

And he knew it, too. Indeed, in less guarded moments, Michael sounded pretty devastated. 'I'll go home and I'll curl up in a ball and I'll cry,' he told one interviewer. 'I'm not kidding. I'll just cry.' But there was an upside – at least the pain made him more creative. 'I'm really sentimental. That's why I think I love the music that I love,' he said. 'It's always tough to end a relationship, isn't it? It helps me actually to write. Whatever I'm going through, it's usually helpful.'

And so Michael set out to write 'I Just Haven't Met You Yet', while he described what he wanted in a woman. 'I don't want a pushover,' he said. 'I want a strong human being that doesn't put up with my BS. It turns me on actually.' In fact, that's pretty much exactly what he'd had with Emily. No wonder he was beside himself with grief.

Heartbroken he might have been, but Michael wasn't going to be without female company for long: shortly after the split, he was photographed kissing the American singer Heather Fogarty. But again, it was Emily who really appeared to be moving on. Towards the end of 2008, she was being increasingly seen with the actor John Krasinski, and the two were spotted sharing a romantic break in California, leading to rather licentious reporting of the news. 'They ordered room service, took long walks and spent every second together,' an observer to it all told *Star* magazine. 'John really cares for Emily – he totally fawns over her. And she's loving the attention. She's a down to earth girl, but it's nice to be treated so well.'

Was that a dig at Michael? Was she trying to make a point?

Both Michael and Emily had always been keen to emphasise how normal and down to earth they were, but perhaps Emily was beginning to want someone who would make a bit of a fuss. She was a big star now, after all, and might have wanted her partners to recognise this. Certainly, it was Michael who seemed to have lost out – not her.

But then again, perhaps the two did just grow apart. Michael was already at the top of one show business tree and Emily was making her way swiftly up another one. Perhaps neither felt they could sacrifice any more of themselves and their career to address a relationship that had once seemed so right. But although they had been together three years, compared with the seven he'd spent with Debbie, there seemed to be a sadness surrounding Michael post-split that there had never been before.

Michael is an artist though, and like all great artists uses his personal experiences in his work. It is said that Frank Sinatra didn't become a truly great torch singer until he'd loved and lost Ava Gardner, after which his voice took on a quality it had never quite had before. The same will doubtless be true of Michael. He loved, lost – and became a deeper and more complex man.

9

Call Him Irresponsible

It was in 2007, when Michael's relationship with Emily was still going strong, that his third album (not counting the three self-produced ones), *Call Me Irresponsible*, so called, according to Michael, because, "it sums me up", came out. As before, a great deal was riding on this. He may have been far more established than he was when the first two appeared, but the more Michael gained, the more he had to lose. The higher he climbed, the further he had to fall. The downside of success is that people's expectations become all the greater, and Michael knew he was going to have to give it his all. Failure at this stage of the game would have a far more deleterious effect than it would have done earlier. If he hadn't succeeded with his first album, he would probably be back in Vancouver working as a television reporter, or indeed, on his father's boat. It would have been disappointing, but he would have known that he had given it his all.

Now, with not one but two hugely successful albums

behind him, a job on that boat would be a disaster. Michael respected hardworking, working-class men as much as anyone and had nothing but contempt for anyone who put them down, but that simply wasn't his world any more. He could and did make a huge effort to keep his feet on the ground, but he was an international star and to lose that would have been devastating. More was riding on this album than had ridden on anything he had ever done before.

Indeed, despite having seen his life and career transformed over the last few years, Michael was taking nothing for granted. 'At no point have I celebrated the success of the last two records and nor will I celebrate the success of this one, if it's successful,' he told one interviewer in the period leading up to the album's release. 'The second it comes out I'll go to work, I'll tour. And my mind is already on the next record. Coming up with great ideas.' He had experienced success now and had no intention of letting it go. 'I just don't think I can afford to get lazy. You do as well as you want to,' he explained. But he still had that earthy sense of humour, revealing in one promotional interview that a gay fan had been phoning his hotel room from the hotel's lobby. 'I told him I'd come down there and hit him,' said Michael. 'Not because of what he wanted to do to me but because he was phoning my room at that time in the morning.'

The constant touring was a necessity, to keep his name out there in lights, but Michael was used to it now. In 2005, he'd surpassed himself, travelling around the world more than a dozen times, but it was essential, and he knew it. He loved it, too. For a start, the places he was playing were pretty different from the smoky dives he'd started out in. And then there was the sheer adrenalin of being up there on stage. Within every performer, no matter how self-confident, there is something that needs to be loved, and that was no different with Michael. Once out there, with the roar of the audience in his ears, the adulation and the sheer happiness on their faces, real life seemed a million miles away. Who needed external stimulants when you had something like that waiting out there for you? Michael was simply born to perform.

But that didn't take away from the fact that the pressures were getting greater all the time. There was just so much to lose. Then there was the fact that Michael was now a wealthy man. He had not been extravagant and flashed his cash around, but even so, he did have a certain standard of living to maintain these days. And he had been generous with his money, too, giving some of it to his family in order to help them have a very comfortable lifestyle. 'They are classy people and they were shocked,' said Michael. 'But some people don't do it. I have friends who are rich, famous guys and they hoard – I find that a bit strange.'

But it meant that his family, too, would be affected if things were to go wrong for him. While not taking Michael for granted themselves, they had hugely benefited from his success. It wasn't just the money, it was the lifestyle: the international travel, the fact that they, too, were rubbing shoulders with the great and good – if Michael lost that, so would they. The ramifications of what his success had brought him and the consequences of a slide in his career, would not merely hit Michael. The whole Bublé clan would feel the changes in his lifestyle.

And so, a good deal was resting on *Call Me Irresponsible*. The decision was thus taken to develop what Michael had been doing, rather than stick with the same formula he had used before. The new album was slightly different from his previous offering, in that it contained two original numbers rather than just the one, and for the first time could possibly be classed as pop rather than jazz. It was a gamble: Michael had, after all, built his career on being one of a new generation of crooners of the old classics, not as a pop star, and there was at least a danger that his established fans would not like what they heard.

It was a gamble, though, that his record company was prepared to take (although it was also noticeable that the album title referred to one of the classics, not one of the more recent numbers on the CD). The tracks were: 'The Best Is Yet To Come', 'It Had Better Be Tonight', 'Me and Mrs Jones' (courtesy of Emily), 'I'm Your Man', a Leonard Cohen classic, 'Comin' Home Baby', 'Lost', his song for Debbie, 'Call Me Irresponsible', Eric Clapton's number 'Wonderful Tonight', 'Everything', his song to Emily, 'I've Got The World On a String', 'Always On My Mind', 'That's Life', 'Dream', 'L.O.V.E.' and 'Orange Colored Sky'. It was officially released on 1 May 2007, while the first single from the album, 'Everything', debuted at number three on the Canadian BDS airplay charts, the highest debut ever on that chart.

To many observers of the music scene, this album appeared to be a sign that Michael was beginning to take charge of his whole career. David Foster was still very much his guiding hand, but Michael was becoming quite a presence in his own right, too. He had a much bigger input now: 'With this album, I said to David over and over again, "Growth without alienation,"' he related. 'Give the audience the odd bit of cheese, but let's not step over the line. Foster's a genius like I'll never be but his instinct as an executive is to play safe, give the audience what they know they want, and I want to take it to another level. Growth without alienation. If we just keep giving them the same thing, why will they keep buying it?'

And he was certainly sticking up for himself now. 'David wanted me to do Chris de Burgh's "Lady In Red" on this album,' he continued. 'I said, "David, I love you man, but I cannot go there." I wouldn't be able to listen to my own record. So we did "Me and Mrs Jones", which was a compromise, which works wonderfully. I have my own cheesy ideas, but there's a line my instincts say I must not cross. I want to stick around, and that means pleasing, but, even as you sing schmaltz, you have to develop, you have to be fresh, but you have to do it without losing your audience, by taking them with you.'

His instincts were becoming increasingly important. It was Michael, not his record label, who had a close relationship with his fans: it was he who saw them out in the audience as he stood up on stage, he who received the fan mail, he who got mobbed after the concerts, and he who knew what they really, really liked. And so he really was the right person to think about what should be going on the new album – always guided by wiser, more experienced hands, of course. It was in everyone's interest for Michael to have a growing input into the work now: the record company bosses knew that as well as anyone.

And so everyone prepared for the new album's release. Various events took place in the run-up to it all. Michael stood in for Tony Bennett, with whom he had duetted on *Duets: An American Classic*, to sing 'Call Me Irresponsible' on *American Idol* season six. This was, in fact, one of the few events in the run-up to the release of the album that did not go strictly as intended: Michael seemed uncharacteristically awkward, stilted even, and at times so ill at ease some people speculated that he'd had a few drinks – or worse. Michael was a little defensive after the event. 'Who, me?' he declared to one interviewer. 'What was I on? Why would they say that? Oh, man. Sure I was disappointed with myself for that performance, but I'd done a video for my new single the day before, I was doing a song live I've never done before in front of thirty-five million people, and I'm covering for the greatest singer ever and, to be honest, I'm terrified. My mother rang me after and said I looked very nervous but seemed to relax more as it went along.'

That was a rare blip: the rest went very much according to plan. Michael's fanclub, Bungalow B, got an exclusive preview of the album and the video for 'Lost', and when it was released, the album went in at number two on the *Billboard* 200, before hitting the number one slot the following week. Michael thus joined a very select group: the only other artists who have managed the same feat are Michael Jackson, Mary J. Blige, Hilary Duff, NWA and Sugarland.

Various other records were broken: in Australia, Michael went on to achieve the highest sales for an album by an international artist for 2007; he also became the first artist in Australia to sell over 30,000 records in a week for two weeks in a row. In the UK, where Michael has a very strong fan base, *Call Me Irresponsible* went on to sell over 300,000 copies, with the special edition version selling over 462,000. It became the eighteenth best selling album of 2007 in the UK.

Any doubts in either Michael's mind or that of his record company that he was a two-trick pony were thus utterly laid to rest: had he sat down and asked for a particular reception for the record, he couldn't have done better than this one, and given both that he had a far greater input to this album than he had the previous ones and that this one was taking a slightly poppier direction, it was all grist to the mill. He was succeeding not only in the eyes of his record company, but on his own terms. Michael really was getting where he wanted to go.

But just how much further was Michael going to be able to go? After the triumph of *Call Me Irresponsible*, it was beginning to look possible that he just might have it in him to become one of the all-time greats himself. And in this, his choice of music stood him in good stead. There are some notable, obvious and huge exceptions to the rule, but people who sing the old classics have tended to have a longer innings than pop stars. For every Rolling Stones, there are a hundred groups who were the big thing of their day, and it gets even harder to think of individual singers who have lasted throughout the years. Madonna is one, the very different Cliff Richard another and the even more different Barry Manilow a third. But there aren't many of them. The Rat Pack, on the other hand, went on for years.

A case in point was Michael's great hero Tony Bennett, who, after all, was well into his eighties and still singing. Was Michael going to be able to manage that? 'I can't see it, but then at this point it's hard even to project forward to being forty,' said Michael extremely cautiously. 'That said, and I hope this won't sound pretentious, I do feel a duty to the vocalists who've inspired me and to those writers responsible for what's termed the Great American Songbook to help keep this music properly alive, not just ticking over on a respirator. I want it to be in the contemporary mainstream, not some museum piece.'

He didn't sound pretentious; he did, however, sound careful. It would have been reckless in the extreme to forecast a career with Bennett's success: a hostage to fortune if ever there was one. But to an outsider charting his career, this was now beginning to look achievable. Michael was no longer a one-off or even two-off success: it had got to the stage that when he brought out a new album, it was an event. People were curious to know what he was doing and what his next move would be. A new Michael Bublé album was becoming something to look forward to, both for his fans, who loved the music, and his record company, which was making a great deal of money. Everyone was a winner where Michael was concerned.

He was also very aware of the importance of his live performances. It wasn't just the records that had to be great: everything else that went into his career had to be perfect, too. 'Look, man,' he told one interviewer, 'even if people are not much into the music, they think I'm bubble gum, I want them to think of me as someone who puts on a hell of a show. I know that men are often dragged to my show against their will. I want them to come up at the end of the show, look me in the eye, and say, "Shit, good on you, man."' There was, incidentally, in that comment just a trace of the boy who'd wanted to fit in. Of course Michael wanted to be congratulated for his artistic undertaking. But he couldn't help but want to be one of the boys, too.

Indeed, he admitted as much when recalling the early days of his career. Asked if he'd thought, at the beginning, that his career would take off in the way it did, he was incredulous. 'Honestly?' he asked. 'Honestly? At first, I just thought it might get me laid. Being sixteen, singing "Come Fly With Me" and "Under My Skin", it gave me a weird kind of power, the power of sex. I would be singing in nightclubs and there were women and I'm not just a dork among dorks at high school. I was different.' It was clear that he was beginning to relax about the early years, too. Whereas at the beginning, he'd evinced a near despair at being the musical backdrop to suburban lushes, now he could see it for what it was: an entrance into a whole new world.

More than ever, though, Michael was having to learn how to deal with his fans. Jokes about gay guys apart, Michael was finding that being in the public eye could be difficult, especially when everyone wanted a part of you. And it wasn't just the fans who could step totally out of line: as he had already discovered, the paparazzi were known to fling insults in the hope of getting a reaction, which could make it very difficult for a person under pressure to keep his cool. While experiences along the lines of Q magazine were well in the past, Michael's every move was under scrutiny and just one slip-up could make him look very bad in the public eye.

But he was being sensible and watched to see how other people dealt with it all. Tony Bennett gave him some good advice: 'Don't respond, ever, to anything.' Michael had also bumped into none other than Paris Hilton at one point and was very impressed by how she held herself: 'Even when people were totally out of line, grabbing at and mauling and being rude to her, she never showed attitude or was ever less than gracious. I was so impressed and am trying to learn from that,' Michael said. The days of being rude to air stewardesses were well and truly behind him. Michael was learning that with power comes responsibility and he was becoming more powerful by the day.

Indeed, with the Q magazine fiasco some years behind him now, Michael was beginning to relax again a little in the company of journalists. He would certainly never go for a night out on the tiles with them again, but he was able to tease a little. And although he himself was always complaining about his propensity to put his foot in his mouth, the real Michael, the rather earthy, goofy Michael was still coming through loud and clear. He had not had to suppress his personality or put on a straitlaced show to maintain his popularity – his fans loved him because he sometimes came out with, frankly, rather silly remarks. Fame certainly hadn't spoiled him or brought out a more po-faced side.

Now that the album was out, successful and storming up charts all over the world, Michael could start to relax about that, too, and talk a little about what had gone on behind the scenes, and could laugh at himself and everyone involved with it all. The usual planning and, indeed, horse trading, had gone into it. 'He [Michael's manager] wanted to call it *The Real Deal*,' Michael revealed. 'I said, "Are you joking?" But I love him dearly. He's supported me all the way through and I wouldn't be where I am without him, but *The Real Deal*? That's the sort of title that will come back and bite you. It's just setting yourself up to be knocked down.' He may have been right, but there was a distinct note of caution that continued to emerge every time he talked about his career: he may well himself have still been finding all this success almost too good to be true.

But he was prepared to reveal a fascinating insight into the mechanics of putting an album together. Forget the title: the music had been carefully chosen, too. There were a couple of original songs on the album, but Michael was adamant he wanted to go no further than that. 'With success you can become self-indulgent, I wouldn't be happy singing all originals,' he said. 'It's just not me. Maybe that'll bite me in the butt, but my passion comes from interpreting the greatest songs ever written.'

As for the mix as a whole – 'I can relate to them,' said Michael. 'The album's about something like love or heartbreak or the girl that got away.' In that, too, he harked back to the Rat Pack, Frank mourning his lost Ava and the lot of them winning and then losing the girl. But these were universal themes that anyone in any country could relate to and Michael was right: while the songs might have come from different eras and, in two cases, have been self-penned, they did all tap into a universal psyche. Michael was speaking to the hearts of his fans, quite as much as their minds: it was the secret of why he was doing so stunningly well.

And more and more, he explained, Michael was making his own decisions about what went on the record and what he wanted to do. At the time of his first album he had very much done what he was told: by this stage he was calling the shots. 'Yes, producers and people at the record company are still trying to control what I do, in some instances very heavily,' he said in one interview. 'I understand they're just trying to do what they think is right and I love that they give me advice, I really do. I'm hungry for their wisdom and knowledge. But it's my face on the CD sleeve and me who wins or loses as a result of what I put out. Having listened, watched and learnt, I now know exactly who I am and what I want to do.'

And again, now that he had considerably more power himself than he had done previously, Michael was able to look back at his earlier offerings with a more critical eye. That first album with David Foster, for example. Michael had hinted in the past that he'd had reservations about it all and now came out and said so – while at the same time conceding that David had been right. 'I had never heard production like it, so I was prepared to look past the schmaltz,' he said. 'I can joke about it now – I tell David it's the crap first album – but people love schmaltz and there's nothing wrong with schmaltz, within reason. Schmaltz can be great. Look at

Lionel Richie. You can move millions of people with real feeling without getting too deep and troubling.'

Michael was prepared to become involved in controversy as well. The downloading of music from the internet, especially illegal downloading, was a pretty marginal worry as far as most people were concerned, but it was a central issue to the music industry and one that artists had to approach with a certain amount of care. But Michael was also characteristically blunt about the profession he was working in, accepting the difference that the internet had made, and the fact that it was more important than ever before for musicians to put out quality products. The days when artists could take a couple of tracks that would be released as a single and fill the rest of the album with lesser tracks were long gone. It was the artists who recognised this who were going to survive, and Michael was one of them.

'The record business is in trouble,' he said. 'It's in decline, not in the happiest place it's been. One reason is too many artists put out shit records. Records where, yeah, there's one or two great singles, the rest is filler. No wonder people went, "I don't want to spend twenty dollars for two songs." No wonder they went to the internet and bought songs for ninety-nine cents. It really was important for me to really passionately believe there were twelve or thirteen really good songs.'

This was a theme he was to return to on another occasion. 'I was trying to come up with thirteen strong tracks because I'm one of those people who is tired of buying a record for one track,' he said. 'Why not just download one single if we hate the rest of the record? If you can get it for free, people are going to try to get it for free,' he continued on the subject of illegal downloads. 'Not that it's right but it makes sense. I'm tired of listening to the record companies bitch and complain about why people are illegally downloading. I'm shocked that record company executives weren't aware of it soon enough. They knew it was happening and nothing was done, and I just think it's bad form to start blaming the people.'

Not only bad form, but pointless, too. Illegal downloading was a fact of life and so was the fact that it was now possible to buy a couple of songs off the internet rather than a whole album. Again, it was the savvy artist who knew this had to be dealt with and a sensible approach was the one taken by Michael: simply raise the quality of the game. Make sure every track was worth listening to and buying an album for, not just two or three. It was a strategy for survival – and again, one that was necessary for anyone who wanted to build a long-term career.

In analysing the industry the way he did, Michael was comprehensively showing himself to be a man of his time. It was ironic, given that he spent such a lot of time defending himself from charges that he was a man from a different era, but it was possible that Michael understood this aspect of the music industry in a way that the record company bosses did not. The reason? His age. The music industry had changed beyond all recognition specifically because of the internet, and record company executives, who tended to be in their fifties and sixties, could be a bit slow to recognise that. Michael, on the other hand, was the same age as his fans and knew exactly how they went about buying their music. He knew that artists were beginning to have to adopt a very different strategy from that which had gone before. But he was rising to the challenge, as were other artists who saw the way that the future was going. Again, this kind of input was invaluable for the record label, and they were smart enough to take it on board.

And, of course, Michael was aware himself that his place in the industry had changed. He was quite touchingly open about it, sometimes sounding more like the young ingénue than an established artist. And he made no bones about what was at stake. 'There's much more to lose now,' he said. 'I'm so excited and so terrified at the same time. I don't want people to hate it. I want them to love it. Every artist's nightmare is to be in the "whatever happened to" file.'

There didn't seem to be much chance of that at the moment. Fans were still marvelling about Michael's voice, which, as he acknowledged, was changing. 'My voice is getting deeper,' he said. 'There's a big tonal difference between twenty-five and thirty-one. I don't know if I'm getting better, but I'm learning what to do with it all – learning from my mistakes. I'm starting to produce now too.' Again, this was pointing to a much longer-term career than had seemed possible in the past. Artists who are also able to write songs, to say nothing of entering into production, have a far bigger say in their own future, as well as increased earning capacity and additional skills to use should their initial areas of expertise dry up. Whether he was doing it wittingly or not, Michael was laying down foundations for a much bigger career than ever he had envisaged before.

And now that he really had got somewhere with his career, Michael was able to take a step back to develop an overview of the last few years. It had been an incredible journey, and he knew that. 'The more I think back, the crazier I was to try what I tried,' he told one interviewer. 'I come from a family of commercial fishermen and my grandfather's a plumber with no musical training. The first music I studied were the duets between Louis Armstrong and Ella Fitzgerald. I was going out with a girl and her parents asked what music I liked. I was trying to impress them so I said, "I love Ella Fitzgerald. He's one of my favourites" – because I thought it was Louise [sic] Armstrong . . . I thought that was the girl in the partnership. I was only thirteen, but I found out later and thought, "What a fool!'"

It was a subject he was increasingly fond of: those childhood days and his own introduction to the music that was standing him in such good stead. All Michael's good humour and lack of pretension came into play: all his ability to laugh at himself and the earnest young boy he once was added hugely to his already extensive amount of charm. Much has been made of his boyish looks, but there was something boyish about his behaviour, as well, for all that he was now a thirty-something mover and shaker in the music business. Michael was clearly one of the many people who have experienced stratospheric success yet find it hard to believe in their good fortune.

Another of the issues that was brought up increasingly was Michael's musical style, specifically the subject of borrowing. Michael was more open than ever about how he had developed his very distinctive voice. 'It's partly stealing,' he said. 'The first time Tony Bennett and I got together we talked about this. I'm so lucky. I get to steal the life's work of my idols – it's an honour. Ella Fitzgerald, Bennett and Bobby Darin. Presley and Sinatra. I can steal all these things I love like the dulcet quiver Dean Martin has.' Of course, he might call it stealing, but another way of looking at it was that he was learning from the greats. Apart from the music lessons Grandpa Mitch had paid for when Michael was a kid, he had not, after all, had any formal training, and this was his way of making up for it. To study the great exemplars of the music you cherish is not pinching their technique and then pretending it is your own: it is studying the masters. Michael was wise to follow the path he did.

He was also putting his life experience into his work. At the time his relationship with Emily was a happy one, but he admitted that the number 'Always On My Mind' brought back memories of Debbie. 'I was very afraid of that song,' he told one interviewer. 'I had a lot of guilt, to be honest with you. I was on the edge. I don't think I opened my eyes the whole time I was singing it.' Perhaps not, but his personal experience did give him an edge he would otherwise not have had: like any great artist his life and art had become intertwined.

Michael had by now got even more into the habit of taking his family with him on tour: it gave him company when he was on the road away from Emily, and it gave them a great trip. Like he himself, Michael's family had not had a great deal of chance to travel until now, and they were thrilled that their famous offshoot was allowing them to see the world.

They were seeing it in some style, as well. Just as he enjoyed being able to give his family some financial support, so Michael was delighted to see how much they enjoyed this aspect of life with him. 'It means much more to me seeing how thrilling it is for them, especially my grandpa,' said Michael. 'They think it's the greatest thing, having a late breakfast then a stroll around whichever new city we're in. Later on there'll be some dinner in advance of the show and they'll start having a few pops. In fact, I doubt if they're totally sober at any point, but they don't need to be. They're on holiday.' Michael, however, was hard at work, determined to consolidate the success of the last few years and do even better than he had done before.

But why was he doing quite as well as he was? Michael had

talent, obviously, a beautiful voice, a hard work ethic and charisma. But other performers had these qualities, too, and they hadn't got to where Michael was now. Just what did he have that the others didn't? It was a subject Michael himself had often thought about.

'I think there's a bravado, which comes from insecurity,' he said. 'I'm like everyone, I go through different moods, sometimes arrogant and cocky, other days demure and self-conscious, really shy. Honestly? I don't know who I am. They keep asking me to play myself on TV shows and I can't really do it. How can I play myself when I don't know who the hell I am?'

Indeed. But did it really matter? Whoever Michael was, in his own eyes or anyone else's, he was doing spectacularly well and his fans loved him for it. And, career-wise, at least, it could only get better from here. He was in a different league, now, the über league that only the very fortunate and the very talented get to experience. At times he'd thought he'd never experience what was now his everyday life. But he was wrong. He'd made it. He was there.

10

The Pressures of Fame

It was beginning to sink in that he'd done it again. Michael Bublé's third album had been a staggering success: his future, at least for now, was assured. Michael appeared to have the world at his feet: what could possibly go wrong now? Well — everything. It is part of the human condition that as soon as matters seem to be going well, the individual concerned is overcome by fear that now it is all bound to go wrong again. So it was with Michael. He had had such good luck: surely it was now time for it all to go horribly, badly wrong?

'I think it has been more of a pressure,' Michael admitted to one interviewer, in the wake of the album's release. 'I wake up some mornings and think God has blessed me, I'm very good at what I do. And the next morning I think, "My God, I'm not fooling anyone, I'm a complete fraud." I'm insecure and my confidence goes back and forth; one day I'm the king, the next I'm a pauper. It's a tough business. It's a slog, but it's work that I love. It's funny, though, with this record I wanted to take more risks. I think I've made it eccentric and, at the same time, palatable.'

There are all kinds of problems and temptations a performer has to face at different stages in his or her career, all kinds of pressures and all kinds of issues that would have seemed almost unbelievable only a few years previously. That was very much the case with Michael now. There were sales figures to worry about, industry profiles to maintain, record bosses to keep happy, and on top of that the incessant pressure of touring to keep the whole show on the road. It is at this stage of some performers' careers that real problems start to emerge, specifically with drink and drugs, for fame is a many-headed beast and can snap at or even devour the unwary. It didn't happen to Michael. While he was happy to talk about his insecurity, at the same time, he had that very solid family behind him, not only to keep his feet on the ground but to help him deal with something that might have taken its toll in other ways, had they not been there. Michael had already been through his 'Do you know who I am' phase and so was able to recognise any incipient signs of misbehaviour on his own part. He had been disgusted with the way he behaved in the past: he had no wish to go back there again.

Even so, there was a rare bout of public bad temper in January 2007. Having been nominated for a Grammy for Best Traditional Pop Vocal Album for *Caught in the Act* – one of his fellow nominees was Tony Bennett, along with Sarah McLachlan, Bette Midler and Smokey Robinson – Michael caused outrage by lashing out at the awards ceremony because his category wasn't televised and by saying that he wasn't going to win. 'They give away our Best Traditional Pop award at a dinner before the Grammys, so I just think that's bullshit,' he said. 'I think it's absolute crap. Our category is now selling way too many records to be given away at a dinner before, so I'm just not going to show up. Why should I go to the Grammys? Because I'll lose . . . They might as well have already scratched Tony Bennett's name into the damn thing. I'm not going. I'm on that record that I'm going to lose to, and it'll be the second year in a row that I've lost. I'm not going to go.'

Was it sour grapes? Perhaps a bit. Michael seemed to be lashing out on all sides, complaining he felt 'like a dirtbag' on the red carpet and saying he wasn't recognised, 'just because I'm not in the tabloids. You just get pukey with it. It's like, enough. No.'

It was an indication of the depth of his feelings that he was prepared to lash out at his idol and friend Tony Bennett, and now he even dragged Emily into it. Emily had recently won Best Supporting Actress at the Golden Globes, something Michael had been ecstatic about at the time, but now he was even feeling bad-tempered about that. 'When she won the thing, I was outside having a cigarette,' he snapped. And instead of going to the Grammys, 'I'm going to stay home and watch the [Vancouver] Canucks. I got to meet Roberto Luongo [Vancouver Canucks' goalkeeper] and his wife. They're going to come over for dinner at my grandma's and stuff and that to us is like the craziest we get.'

This was not typical of Michael. It was unlike him to be ungracious, especially where Emily was concerned – and indeed, Tony Bennett – but the pressures were beginning to tell. He might have been an unknown until relatively recently, but he was nominated for the Grammys now, and if he was being made to feel an also-ran, he was going to let the world know about it. As it happens, common sense prevailed and he did attend the award ceremony after all. And – just as he'd predicted – Tony Bennett won for *Duets*. But the media seized on the episode, and Michael was not allowed to forget his outburst for some time to come. It was a salutary lesson that he should be extremely grateful for what he'd been given and one that Michael was not to forget quickly again.

But there were so many potential problems these days. If it wasn't the public, it was his family that might prove a cause for concern. One difficulty that seems to have been avoided, however, is sibling rivalry. Brandee was a teacher, so there was unlikely to be an issue there, but Crystal was also in show business. She was an actress. And while she had done tolerably well, she wasn't in the same league as her famous brother. But the Bublés were not a warm, close-knit family of Italian origin for nothing: Crystal did not display any signs of jealousy – quite the opposite. She seemed well and truly able to cope with the status quo.

'It's OK,' she told one interviewer who had brought up the subject of Michael. It was 2007 at the time, Crystal was best known professionally for her ongoing role in *Cold Squad*, and she had just had a small, independent movie out called *Crossing* (as in double crossing), in which she played a call girl. Michael and Emily attended the premiere and created a sensation – probably more than would have happened for a small Canadian feature film under other circumstances, which in itself could have been galling. But Crystal was pretty cool. 'He's kind of famous,' she said. 'There actually was a time when I made more money than him.'

But the Bublé common sense was there, as well as the humour, and a profound awareness of what was really important in life. For all his massive fame and success, unlike his two sisters, Michael had not been able to form a really lasting relationship. They were both married; he was still single. And the

Bublé parents wanted that kind of happiness and stability for all their children. They were certainly doing everything in their power to make it come about. There had been that very publicly stated desire for Michael to marry Emily, and tellingly, perhaps, it was Lewis and Amber who had introduced their daughter to her husband Lanny. Originally a fisherman, he had become a mortgage broker, and Crystal – unlike her brother – had a rock-solid personal life.

But still. To be the sister of a superstar! Indeed, Crystal was as good-humoured as the rest of her family about what had happened. Roger Larry was the film's director and originally cast it in 2002, just before Michael made his breakthrough: 'Michael who?' he thought. 'I can't commit to anything,' he told Crystal. 'But if you give me a demo, I'll take a listen.' It was a good call: by the time the film had come out, Michael had gone stratospheric and Larry was realistic enough to understand that could only be good news for the movie itself.

Of course, Crystal had been watching her brother's rise to the stratosphere and was mature enough to see the downside, too. That furore over the Grammys had not been pleasant to watch. 'Am I freaked out?' she said. 'Absolutely. It scares me. To be taken out of context like he was, I don't think it's fair. It's scary because we're not perfect. We can't always know the right or smart thing to say. When I see his life, I think, "Wow, I'm glad you're doing it because I couldn't. It's crazy." I'm very happy with the way my life is right now. If I can just work quietly and go home, I'd be very, very happy.'

And anyway, there was always the music. Michael was thoroughly enjoying talking about it all. The third album was still very much on his mind: sometimes he seemed as excited as a child when he talked to interviewers about what he'd been doing. For a start, there was his hook-up with Henry

Mancini, best known for creating the *Pink Panther* score, in the number 'It Had Better Be Tonight' (Meglio Stasera), which had actually been written for the original *Pink Panther* film. 'At first, I thought how can a 31-year-old guy from Canada get together with one of his idols, a 61-year-old Brazilian, [Michael was mistaken – Mancini was actually another Italian-American] and sing the song from completely different aspects? But it means the same to both of us. Love is love, you know,' said Michael happily. Anyway, it was a very nice link-up to have: Mancini was a huge name in film scores, the *Pink Panther* theme probably, along with James Bond, the most famous ever written. And despite Michael's oft-repeated avowal that he was a child of his own times, not the mid-twentieth century, he did have the aura of a sophisticate about him that this music suited very well.

He was also rather enjoying talking about 'Lost'. All right, so it might have stemmed from a rather painful part of his life, but that was well and truly over now and Michael was thoroughly enjoying being a composer as well as a singer. 'It was my comment on the state of my life,' he explained to one interviewer. 'Love is either one way or the other. You're in it big time or you're out of it big time. You're glowing and smiling or you're devastated and in tears. Or at least that's how it is for me. I'm an all-or-nothing person.'

He could say that again and there was something very engaging about Michael, as he pranced about like a puppy, constantly praising his beautiful girlfriend Emily. But there was also, did he but know it, a slightly ominous note about it all. 'I believe the only time relationships with men and women work is when a man loves the woman more,' he declared. 'That's how it works with me. I know my mother and father are in love, but my dad is gaga over my mum and she plays it coy. So I'm happy to say, I'm the one who's more in love.' He was about to find out the truth of that faster than he could have imagined. Post-split, Emily was the cool one, the one who recovered pretty quickly. It was Michael who appeared publicly devastated, an image he hasn't entirely shaken to this day.

But while Michael liked to talk about Michael the lover, he was also always careful to make sure that people saw the other side of him, too. This was the Michael who was a regular guy, who might have been the crooner who made 'em swoon, but who was also a red-blooded Canadian with no fancy airs and graces and a healthy disregard for nonsense and namby-pamby ways. He was still the fisherman's son. 'At home, I don't sit around in suits with my hair all done,' he declared. 'I'm more likely to be sitting around in my underwear eating from a bag of nachos and watching TV. Emily says, "If your friends could see you now, you nerd!" I flirt on stage and in real life. I flirt with everyone – men and women. I'm not a smarmy flirt, though. I'm harmless. People think I'm soft because I sing romantic songs but I'm a regular guy – I like sport and beer.'

This dual side of his personality could come out in different ways. In the UK to promote the record, Michael gave an interview to one lady journalist, who did what an awful lot of British lady journalists do when presented with a superstar heartthrob and pretended the interview was some sort of a date. She brought Michael a rose, and asked him to pose with it. 'No way,' said Michael. 'That's so cheesy and clichéd. I'm not doing that.'

You could hardly blame him. The interviewer professed herself to be greatly disappointed, but it's hard to see what else Michael could have done. He was constantly wary about being set up these days, either to be made to look foolish, or to look as if he was chatting up someone else, on top of which he had a girlfriend he was besotted with. It's hardly surprising that caution was the order of the day.

He did relax a little after that: 'I'm not at the "being mobbed" stage, but it would be kinda nice,' he continued to the interviewer. 'Women don't throw their knickers at me on stage. You shouldn't take yourself too seriously. I want people to know I can take the piss out of myself and just have a laugh. I want to relate to the guys in the audience, too. I just want to entertain people.' (It should be noted, as well, that his words were a direct riposte to a comment Emily had given about women doing exactly that, throwing knickers on the stage. It had all the hallmarks of a joke bantered between the two of them.)

But still his regime was very hard work. There was no let-up in the sheer amount of travelling Michael had to do, even now that he was at the top of the tree. He told another interviewer just after his arrival in London that he couldn't remember where he'd jetted in from – 'Isn't that horrible?' he said. And he was off again immediately afterwards, although he wasn't quite sure where – 'I don't want to see my schedule,' he continued. 'It's the only way I can do it without feeling overwhelmed. It's tough not to panic when you've got to be in fifteen countries in three weeks. [But] I want this still as badly today as I ever did. At the end of the day, if I don't do the publicity, I'm only shooting myself in the foot.'

In that way, as in many others, Michael was a publicist's dream. Not only had it not gone to his head: he was aware that all the fame and adulation could vanish in a minute, and he was prepared to work as hard as anyone to make sure that didn't happen. Again, all those years of slogging away stood him in very good stead. It is only when you have had to work very hard indeed to achieve what you want that you realise how much you want it, and indeed, how hard you are prepared to go on working in order to maintain it. Michael had certainly realised that now. And so the slog continued: one flight after another, one country after another, one concert after another. It was definitely as well that Michael had his family on hand to help him cope with it all.

At times, Michael almost seemed to be disillusioned by his success, which, despite all its rewards, is hardly surprising given the workload involved. They say it is better to travel than to arrive: he certainly sounded, at times, as if that was the way he felt. 'The journey is way better than reaching the goal,' he told one interviewer. 'There was a wonderful beauty waking up every morning and having a goal that you live for. These days I don't have the desperation that I had. I love my life, I get to do what I love in front of people all over the world, but there's not the same burning.'

Was it that that had driven him to recklessness in the midst of a relationship with the woman he loved – the fact that life now seemed a smidgen too easy? Is that why he, like so many men, destroyed what he wanted, his relationship with Emily, above all? It is hard not to speculate that if true then it was a moment of madness with some, perhaps subconscious, desire to inject an element of danger into a life that was now so full in so many other ways. If that's right, then Michael was certainly to pay a high price for the infusion of illicit excitement into his life.

Yet another aspect of his life that Michael had never really had to worry about before, but which was now a big issue, was preconception. People now had a pretty firm view in their head about Michael Bublé, whether they had met him or not, and Michael could sometimes find this a little wearisome, too. 'People meet me and they think I'm going to be brooding and serious,' he told one interviewer. This was not, however, quite true. 'If you ask me something, I'll tell you – and I have a really dry sense of humour,' he protested. That serious image was in part due to his publicity shots and album covers. They did tend to feature Michael looking rather soulful: his handsome Italian-American features often bathed in strategic shadow, the look on his face that of a man dealing with the great issues of life, love, loss and music. And anyway, there were considerably worse misconceptions that people might have had – that he was going to be a jerk, or an asshole, say.

He had to be the lover boy, too. Michael was a heartthrob, and people expected him to behave like a heartthrob. He might have wisely managed to avoid posing with roses, but people still looked to him to play the role of the Italian lover, and that was not a look that involved appearing to tell jokes. However, his appearance on his album covers and publicity shots was totally different from that on stage: on the former he appeared soulful, and on the latter he was constantly larking around, still chatting up the women and sympathising with the men for having to be there. Anyone who actually spent time with him knew that the reality was goofiness and a ribald sense of humour. But people expected to see Michael the lover, and so Michael the regular guy was constantly having to cope with surprise that he was not what people were expecting at all.

Another sign that Michael was now a member of the showbusiness establishment, rather than one of the hopefuls queuing up in the corner, came when *The X Factor* in the UK started airing in autumn 2007. One of the contestants, Leon Jackson, cited Michael as one of his major influences, and indeed, his major experience of singing before coming on the show had been singing along with Michael's albums. He had 'grown up' listening to Michael, he explained, which must have been pretty bizarre to Michael given that he'd only hit the big time a couple of years previously. But Leon was nineteen and Michael was thirty-two, a huge gap in years at that particular stage in life, and Leon's perspective of time was quite different from that of his idol. It was a graphic representation of a generation who really had grown up listening to Michael, unaware that for Michael himself, some aspects of his life now still seemed relatively new.

Now Leon was out in public himself, quite as excited as the young Michael had been when he first started to make his way in the world. 'My mum used to tell me I could sing,' said Leon, who was also a black belt in karate. 'But I never sang at school, apart from doing hymns, because I didn't have the confidence. I only started doing karaoke this year. That's why it was such a shock to get through on *X Factor*. I just didn't expect it. Louis [Walsh] told me I was his favourite act in Scotland. I couldn't believe it. And Sharon [Osbourne] said it was rare to see someone with such raw talent. It was such a brilliant feeling, I was completely blown away by the reaction. I haven't got much experience but I know now I can sing.' He duly made it through to the finals.

There was a huge amount in the press about all this: not just Leon himself, although he attracted plenty of attention, having been brought up by a single mother in West Lothian, but also about the fact that he was such a big fan of Michael's. Michael hardly needed the publicity, but it was gratifying, nonetheless: an up-and-coming young singer professing such admiration could only make him look good, in addition to emphasising quite how far his own career had come. In the event, it went one step better for Leon Jackson: he got to duet with Michael live on stage at Wembley. Leon was clearly thrilled. 'I'd never rehearsed it with him, and I never had a sound check – just went up and winged it and it was beautiful,' said a rather breathless Leon, who also went backstage to meet Emily and the Bublé family. 'It's just incredible because I've grown up listening to Michael Bublé. If *The X Factor* ended now, I'd still be so happy. Whenever I get depressed I'll always remember that experience and it will bring myself back up.'

Leon was certainly enjoying his moment in the sun, Bublé-related and otherwise. 'Every week that goes by is just amazing, and looking back it's hard to pick a highlight. It may be between meeting Girls Aloud and performing at Wembley this week with my idol, Michael Bublé. I've been so lucky with the stars that have been on the show – I still can't believe it.' *X Factor* judge Louis Walsh also had his tuppence worth to put in: 'Leon has potential to be a total star,' he said. 'He is as good a vocalist as Michael Bublé.' What Michael himself thought about the young pretender being put on a par with him has not been revealed, but shortly afterwards, Leon went on to win the competition.

Leon had duetted with Kylie Minogue as well, by this time, but there was no hiding who Leon really rated. Michael. 'It was such an amazing experience to sing with him,' said Leon in another interview. 'It was the best buzz of my life – until I won *The X Factor* of course. Me and Michael got on really well so if I can do something with him I'll be made up.' And so it goes: Tony Bennett, with whom Michael had duetted, handing down the baton to the younger man; Michael himself now handing it down to Leon . . . although that is putting it a little too strong. Michael clearly had no intention of handing anything on to anyone just yet. But still, he was, for the first time in his life, the older star showing a younger guy the ropes. It must have been a strange sensation, and in some ways bittersweet.

Leon himself was loving it. Indeed, he was experiencing something of what Michael himself had gone through once fame had kicked in. 'It's been completely insane – I keep having all these women coming up to me and saying, "You're fit,"' said Leon. 'I'm not used to it all but it's really flattering – it's a real confidence boost. I have no problem chatting to girls – they love it when I tell jokes and do impressions.' And like Michael, he wanted to look after his parents, or in this case, parent – his mother Wendy, forty. 'I want to buy my mum a new house because she's been so amazing to me all my life – bringing me up on her own,' he went on. 'She's always provided for me and I always said I wanted to look after her and I will. I'm not really a flash person – I'm quite careful with money.' (Shades of Michael there, too.)

It turned out that, fan as he was, the link with Michael had also been carefully thought out. 'I was well aware when I entered *X Factor* that there were others in the contest who had been doing this for years like Rhydian and Nikki, and I struggled to keep up with them,' said Leon, showing rather more nous about the industry than might have been suspected. 'I was very much the "karaoke kid" who was more used to playing bars full of drunken mobs who did not really appreciate my jazzy style. But my friends told me I had a good voice and I gained the confidence to keep performing. Then I decided to apply for *X Factor*. And now I've gone and won it. From what I have been told, we are going to take our time on what the album will be like. There is no rush. Obviously, my heart lies with jazz. My tone suits that. But on *X Factor*, we went along the Michael Bublé "line" because he has also covered the Beatles, George Michael and Stevie Wonder. I want to make an original album.'

It was quite uncanny in some ways, however, how much he sounded like his idol. Leon wanted to play the same type of music as Michael, was wary about doing too much self-penned material, knew the importance of not letting success go to his head and was also wise enough to wish to avoid the temptations that can be on offer to a young and successful man. 'Jazz is my favourite style and my voice really suits that, but I'm very versatile,' Leon explained. 'I like John Legend, so R&B is an area I want to explore, too. It's going to be an album of original and interesting material that I make. I won't be allowed to get big-headed. I'd get kicked down by my mum or gran if I developed an ego. Because of my upbringing I think my feet are very well on the ground. And I'm a good judge of character, so no one will take advantage of me. Drugs have never been me. I'm not interested. I much prefer a quiet drink and karaoke with my pals.'

Michael was not the grand old man of the music industry: he was still far too young for that. Indeed, still in his early thirties, he would have been taken aback to be regarded as such: for all his comments about it being better to travel than arrive, he still felt he had a great deal more to do, places to go to, people to see. Michael's ambitions had not abated one inch. But he was now a figure to be looked up to: young singers wanted to be the new Michael Bublé, no matter that the old one was still going strong. Younger performers were charting his career, watching how he'd done it and taking points about what they themselves should be doing next. Rather deliciously, given all the charges of copying that had been levelled against him, singers were now looking to Michael to see how best to use their voice.

Another sign of his new status was that other bands were now beginning to cover Michael's songs. It must have been a strange experience, given how much stick he'd taken for performing other people's material in the past, but Michael was now seeing other musicians performing not just the greats that he had interpreted, but even the music he'd written himself. The Irish band Westlife was releasing a cover version of 'Home' in October 2007 and they sounded very like Michael himself when discussing upcoming events.

'It's actually exciting getting back into the studio,' said band member Kian Egan. 'We all have an input into the songs we pick because sometimes one of us will hear something in a song that the others won't. We are not songwriters, we're singers. It would be silly for us to try and write songs when there are people out there that can do a much better job than us.' That was exactly the argument that had been used in the past to defend Michael. He must have experienced a sense of déjà vu as Westlife ran through all the accusations that had also been made against him.

In the event, however, Westlife's version of 'Home' not only did badly (relatively speaking – badly on Westlife terms, in that it was number three after Leona Lewis and Take That) but received a critical mauling, which cannot have been much fun for Michael to observe. It was he, after all, who'd written the song, and Westlife fans, writing on the band's website, were pretty critical of their idols' endeavour.

'The song has to take some of the blame for Westlife not being number 1 on Sunday,' wrote one. 'The only reason I downloaded it is because I thought I should support Westlife. I won't be buying the CD of the single because I will hardly listen to it. It's a cover and not their best at that.'

She was not alone. 'Both [Take That's and Leona's] songs

are original tracks and new to the public,' wrote another. 'I personally don't have a problem with WL releasing covers but Michael Bublé released Home only two years ago. I think it was the wrong song to launch the album.' They were not alone in those sentiments and, unfair as it might have been, Michael's name did not escape unscathed. This was a setback for him, too. Michael had grown used to success and no one likes to be associated with failure, even if one step removed.

Not that Michael appeared too concerned. Towards the end of 2007, he was touring Britain, receiving rave reviews and clearly thoroughly enjoying himself. At one concert, he singled out an eight-year-old in the crowd, pointed at her and commented, 'Without fans like you, cutie pie, I would end up like Amy Winehouse.' He was then set upon by female fans: 'I've never had so many pieces of me grabbed before,' said Michael. His good nature continued to shine through: perhaps the experiences with Leon and Westlife had brought it home to him quite how lucky he was. For while Leon had yet to prove that he would be able to stand the test of time, and while Westlife had to cope with constant speculation that they were splitting up, or griping that the single hadn't done well, Michael was, pure and simple, at the top of the tree.

And he had finally and comprehensively cracked the United States. His previous albums had done OK, but this really was it: apart from performing on *American Idol* and impressing Oprah Winfrey, *Call Me Irresponsible* had debuted at the top of the charts. And it had been a very different journey from the last time round. 'I come in with more experience,' he told one journalist. 'In certain ways I am more confident and in other ways I am far more humble. I realise I have made a lot of mistakes and done things wrong. I've done things I wish I could have done in another way. I didn't come in with the same kind of desperation that I may have had on the first or second record. I didn't come in thinking, "Oh God, please. I hope this does well because I have nothing else and I worked so hard at this." I have come to the point now where I am really allowing myself to enjoy it, really enjoy it.'

He deserved to. But he was learning about himself in other ways, too. Asked what his biggest mistake was, he replied, 'My mouth. I am a candid interview and I have a dark and dry sense of humour – a very Canadian sense of humour and I am only learning now stupidly that you can't read tongue. When I say something funny in a newspaper and I meant it to be funny, it doesn't read that way. It is the same if you have ever gotten an email and you think, "What did I ever do to make this person respond this way?" They never meant to be aggressive, but you can't read the tone. I've said things. There were comments about many things I wish I would have said in a different way or a more eloquent way.'

All told, however, he hadn't done too badly. And he was philosophical about everything else, too. Asked about negative critics, he replied, 'It was to be expected. I am singing a genre of music that people are very protective of. I am being compared to the greatest vocalist of all time. Someone asked me the other day, "Do you get upset when people say you are the young Frank Sinatra?" It doesn't upset me. It is a huge compliment, but it is false. There will never be another Frank Sinatra. I never wanted to be another Frank Sinatra. I only wanted to be another Michael Bublé.

'Maybe one day I will get my revenge and some young kid will come up and you will say, "So what do you think about people calling you the young Michael Bublé?" Hopefully, he'll say, "Bublé sucks." I understand. Every time a new rock singer comes out they don't say, "Are you the new John

Lennon?" Every time a new rapper comes out, it's not, "Are you the new Dre?" I am never sure why this sort of genre, the categorisation is so strong. I have not earned the right to be called the young Sinatra, but give me time.' Give him time, indeed. But there was an irony in that remark, too. Michael could hardly have been better established by this stage. People were beginning to talk about other performers as 'the new Michael Bublé'. Michael had grown used to success and anything else just wasn't good enough.

11

Martini in the Morning

Michael was an established great now himself: proof, if it were needed, was that he was now played regularly on Martini in the Morning, a radio station based in LA that featured the likes of Frank Sinatra, Dean Martin, Harry Connick Jr et al. Michael was one of their number now. He was indisputably one of the establishment, having graduated to that level of über-celebrity in which he got invited on to television to take the mickey out of himself. A case in point was the Australian show *Kath & Kim*, on which he played a role: 'I get to take the piss out of myself, which is fun,' he said. 'It's so cool to be part of something so funny and so self-deprecating.'

Although the split with Emily was coming soon, now, Michael remained extremely close to his family. He spent as much time in Vancouver as he could with them, and would reminisce happily about childhood memories. 'My favourite thing every year was the big trip to the attic to get the Christmas tree in a box and the decorations with my dad,' he recalled. 'I remember the attic smelled musty and was cold and my dad always told me, "Don't touch the insulation – it's not cotton candy." The attic still smells like Christmas to me.' If anything, his family was becoming even more important to him. Try as you might, once you have achieved a certain level of fame, it is simply impossible to keep in touch with the more ordinary side of life and given that Michael couldn't walk down the road without being mobbed, he simply couldn't casually hang out with his friends in the way he once did. But he could hang out with his family, the family that had made him and moulded him and sent him on his way. This was testament to his heritage, too. Michael's Italian-American background was one that lauded the importance of family above all else. Now he really was learning how valuable that was, and how beneficial for him, too.

The change in his status was noted by Canada's newspaper *The Gazette*. In January 2008, it pointed out that five years previously, Michael Bublé had been performing nightly at Le Cabaret Music Hall during the Montreal International Jazz Festival in front of an audience of 300: he was now in the Bell Centre, in front of 15,000, although he certainly wasn't letting that put him off his stride. 'This can, this should, this will be intimate,' he declared, and went on to put on a display of absolutely consummate showmanship, at one point making his way into the audience to have himself photographed with a nine-year-old fan. This was all shown up on the giant monitors: the audience loved it. Indeed, Michael was making quite a thing about picking out very young members of the audience and making a fuss of them: it thrilled them, delighted their parents and made him more popular than ever.

Despite the Westlife experience, more artists wanted to release cover versions of 'Home': the next to do so was the country artist Blake Shelton. Again, Michael showed himself to be generous and welcoming to a fellow artist. Michael was performing at the Sommet Center in Nashville, and Blake was in the audience when Michael – spontaneously and unrehearsed – invited him on to the stage, where the two of them sang the song together. That brought them a standing ovation. It was also, in that it risked Michael being upstaged, a fairly unusual way of going about his working life. But it made his audience love him even more.

It also made him an extremely popular figure among other musicians. 'I was so excited to finally get to meet Michael,' said Blake afterwards. 'He's a great guy, really funny and easy to get to know. When he invited me to sing with him, I was truly honoured and a little nervous since we didn't rehearse. But it was an awesome experience.' It was a very kind gesture on Michael's part, too. The world of entertainment is not known for the generosity its members bestow upon one another and by allowing another artist to share the spotlight like that, Michael was putting himself a step removed from the rest.

He was equally thoroughly nice about it when talking about it elsewhere. 'They're expecting it to go to number one in the country charts,' he said. 'Westlife recorded it, too. Blake's version is so country, but guess what, he's had a bigger hit with it than I ever did.' In actual fact, of course, it was a great compliment that Blake wanted to release the song. Not only was Michael so good that people wanted to cover his songs, but they also wanted the Michael Bublé association. It might not have done Westlife much good, but Michael's name was gold now, and turning to gold just about everything that was associated with it. It was hardly surprising other performers wanted a touch of the Bublé magic of their own.

Another of the advantages of mega-celebrity – for those that choose to put it to good use, at least – is that it can play a genuine role in making other people's lives better. With his increasing involvement in that aspect of it all, Michael was becoming part of the great and good. He had become an ambassador for Hear the World, one of a number of people publicising a charity whose aim was to raise global awareness about the importance of good hearing, and in May 2008, Bryan Adams launched a photography exhibition in New York (from where it was due to travel on to Berlin) featuring those ambassadors. Among the photographs was a particularly charming picture of Michael, seemingly flying through the air, one hand cupped to an ear. There was a palpable sense that, having done so well himself, it was time to give something back. It was to be just one of a growing number of charitable causes to which Michael contributed his name.

Touring continued and it was not always a pleasant experience. 'I had a man try to kill me when I was on tour in America,' Michael told one interviewer. 'I don't think he was well. He was sort of a stalker kind of guy. I think that when the FBI picked him up, he told them that I had "stolen music from black people".' Stalkers – that was yet another problem a person of his stature had to put up with. But it was a small downside compared to what he had accomplished by now. His level of success had so far surpassed his own wildest dreams, that Michael himself sometimes seemed scarcely able to believe that it was all true.

And then, of course, there was Mitch. Sunshine and his grandpa were as close as they ever had been, Grandpa taking as much pleasure in his famous grandson's achievements as Michael did himself. All that early encouragement – all that plumbing he maintained in Vancouver nightclubs just to give his beloved Sunshine a break – had certainly worked out, and then some. And it only enhanced the relationship between the two of them. Could Sunshine have done it without Grandpa? We will never know.

As the superstar life closed in on him, Michael resolutely maintained his status as regular guy. He might be flying by private jet these days, but he refused to put on any airs and graces. And he retained his sense of humour, playing on the notion of the überstar that he actually refused to espouse in real life. 'I'm intolerable,' he said. 'I actually hire someone just to feed me prawn cocktail crisps, one by one. I have to be carried, I don't do stairs any more and I'm also to be called The Maestro whenever people are around. I like to go home and just burn money, sometimes a hundred dollars at a time.'

Indeed, if anything, his sense of humour got even stronger as time went by. He outdid himself at the 2008 JUNO awards, held in Calgary, when he accepted the JUNO Fan Choice Award: 'This is for all those people who said I couldn't vote for myself enough times to win,' Michael commented, before going on to thank the awards' sponsor Dorito 'for making such tasty treats. Sometimes when I eat them, my fingers, they go orange, but it's worth it!'

Once he got started on these flights of fancy, it often seemed as if he couldn't stop himself. Backstage with the press, he went on, 'I do love Doritos. I just learned when you're eating them, you should never watch dirty movies or anything like that. It's true, I thought there was something really wrong with me, but it was just the Doritos.' He let the rest hang in the air, but the implication was plain . . .

This was also the first year that Michael won a Grammy, for Best Traditional Pop Vocal Album. 'Winning a Grammy was a dream come true,' said Michael. 'It was a first for me and

you always remember your first time. It makes it doubly exciting to get back on the road to perform for my fans.' This was
just as well: he spent a huge amount of time in 2008 touring.
He also won two Smooth Jazz awards – Male Vocalist of the
Year and Best Original Composition. It meant a great deal,
obviously, but above all was the simple fact that he'd got there.
He'd made it. He was flying so far above the mass of even very
successful show-business entertainers that he could practically
see the curve of the earth.

His fans, these days, came from everywhere. The UK TV
presenter Paul O'Grady was one of them: 'I love The Bublé,'
he rasped. 'Michael Bublé makes me blush, and no one makes
me blush. He should give lessons in sex appeal. It oozes out of
him. I love him.' Indeed, Michael had made some very enter-
taining appearances on Paul's show. 'You have to . . . stop
loving me so much,' he said on one occasion. Emily was
backstage, taking it all in. Michael started talking about her
fondly, but stopped himself. They were still fighting not to
become a show-business couple. Sadly, of course, in a matter
of months, they would not be a couple at all.

Nor was this the only time 'The Bublé' was the subject of
admiring comment from the stars of British television. On
another occasion, *The Sunday Night Project* was co-hosted by
James Corden, along with regular host Justin Lee Collins. They
loved The Bublé, they declared. Didn't everyone by this stage?
Rarely can a performer have been on such a winning streak.

Michael was cropping up in other parts of the show-
business world, too. Another person celebrating a certain
degree of success in the world of show business was David
Foster. A tribute was to be held for him: a one-night-only live
show called 'David Foster and Friends', which was to take
place at the Mandalay Bay Resort and Casino in Las Vegas.

Michael, of course, was to be one of the performers who took part. Indeed, the round-up as a whole looked very much like an A–Z of the music industry: the performers included Andrea Bocelli, Josh Groban, Kenny G, Boz Scaggs, Katherine McPhee, Babyface, Cheryl Lynn and Blake Shelton, among others too numerous to mention.

It was to be quite a night. 'I am honoured to be recognised in this way by so many of the artists I've had the pleasure of working with over the past three decades,' David Foster said. 'Not only are they supremely talented, but I consider them dear friends, so I'm really looking forward to getting onstage and spending the evening with some of my favourite people in the world.' The fact that Michael was foremost among them was yet another testament to his standing. Just a few years previously, he'd been begging David to take him on. Now he was at the forefront of the roster of some of the most successful names in the world. It meant a lot to both of them: Michael because he was grateful David had taken him on, and David because he was so delighted to see his young protégé make the grade.

The year 2008 flew by in a blur of touring, which must at least have helped dull the shock of splitting up with Emily. Michael had by now sold 20 million records worldwide, with the last album, in particular, making a real stamp on the world. The reviews had been magnificent. 'Michael Bublé's third studio album is the Big One,' said Stephen Holden in the *New York Times*, and the rest of the world seemed to think so, too.

'Bublé's success is defined by his consummate showman-ship,' said the *Montreal Gazette*. 'Whether he's casually gliding down the incline in front of the drum riser, playfully trading insults with his band members or just hanging back to enjoy the whole experience, he's a magnetic presence.'

'It's almost impossible not to keep the beat to a Bublé song,' said the *Wichita Eagle*.

'Bublé puts on "unbelievable" show,' added the *Fort Worth Star-Telegram*.

Over in Britain, everyone was just as starstruck: 'Bublé's stage presence is magnetic,' breathed the *Sunday Times*. 'He has charisma, energy and when he sings, words float out of his mouth; he swivels like Elvis with a flash of a tap dancing Fred Astaire. He has fun.'

As for Australia – 'For the couples in the crowd, his serenades and soothing voice proved to be the perfect mixture for a romantic evening,' the *Reno Gazette-Journal* announced. 'But for everyone in attendance, it would have been hard not to spend the night falling in love with Bublé's style and music.'

Indeed, the Australian lap of the tour was another good illustration of quite how far Michael had come. As the *Sydney Morning Herald* had pointed out, five years previously, Michael had played a one-off showcase at the Basement near Circular Quay. Now he was back with an eighteen-date sold-out tour. Michael certainly seemed to be relishing it: 'It's great to be back in Australia and to have had such an incredible response to the shows so far,' he said. Even his audience was star-studded: among those who'd come out to listen to him were Delta Goodrem and Brian McFadden. He seemed to like Australia: on another occasion, he'd referred to Australians as being very much like Canadians, but with suntans.

There was another element to the Australian tour, too – the ticket prices. Very unusually for an artist of his standing, Michael insisted that the prices were put down, not up. One of the biggest complaints about some stars is quite how much they charge their fans to see them on tour, and Michael wasn't having any of that. 'I had a promoter overseas tell me every ticket would be AUS\$99,' he said. 'I said, "That's not fair, you can't charge ninety-nine dollars if they're in an arena seventy metres away from you." I told [the promoter] Paul Dainty I wanted the ticket prices brought down. My dad called me and said, "Mike, your gross is going to be lower." I'm not saying I don't like making money out of making music, but it's not about the gross of a tour, it's about showing appreciation to an audience.

'It's about letting the guy making thirty grand a year come with his family. It's not going to kill him to bring his family. He bought my record, too, so why should he pay a hundred and fifty dollars for a ticket? If I play theatres, yeah, I get it, it's intimate. But not if I'm an arena act, no way. I'm not so out of touch with reality to not know it's a big deal to come out to a show. If a family comes there's parking, restaurant, babysitters – that all adds up to a lot of money.'

It is hard to overstate quite how unusual this was. Michael was not just playing up to the perception of being a regular guy: he was, quite literally, putting his money where his mouth was. Indeed, he was keen to emphasise that he was still well aware how difficult life could be for other people. 'People are struggling,' said Michael. 'Look at the price of petrol. I've made more money than I ever thought I would, I've sold more albums than I ever thought I would, I want people to know I'm not ripping them off. Some bands charge five hundred dollars a ticket. Who can come to that show? I don't care if Sinatra comes back from the dead, I ain't paying five hundred dollars a ticket. It's nice to build an audience slowly. I still feel like the underdog. Even though maybe I'm not, but I still feel like the underdog.'

It showed a genuine appreciation of the music and the fans that was extremely rare. That was part of the secret of

Michael's popularity: he actually liked his fans and he actually liked doing what he could for them. And it showed he had most certainly not lost touch with his working-class roots. Michael might have been making a lot of money, but he had the nous to realise that most people were not. He also understood that a couple of hundred dollars, while not necessarily meaning a lot to him, still represented a great deal to some people. He was a very unusual performer, to take on board the economics of a situation and say he wasn't going to play ball.

Michael's banter with the audience, meanwhile, was as accomplished as ever. 'I'm not kissing your butts, but this is where the hip people are,' he told a Melbourne audience. 'It's the closest place to my home town of Vancouver.' He staged his customary walk through the crowd, where one rather over-zealous fan gave his bum a hard squeeze: 'There was nothing wimpy about that grab,' said Michael. 'I liked it.'

Indeed, sometimes his stage act seemed to be divided between the younger members of the audience, the ones Michael fought his way into the scrum to be photographed with and then thanked them for not allowing him to be Amy Winehouse, and the older members who took a rather earthier approach to his charms. 'That's a joke, I'm just taking the mickey,' he said of the Amy Winehouse comments. The Bublé trademark humour was making itself felt once more.

'That's the show – I'm cheeky, I'm irreverent, I'm having fun. I know there are points in the show when I'm so dorky it's unbelievable. And see, I met the ten-year-old girl and four seconds later a woman grabbed my ass, so it's all kinda strange. In a weird and probably egotistical way I feel that little kid will never forget that. My dad took me to the Harlem Globetrotters when I was a kid and they picked me to throw this bucket of water. It was a big deal to me. I still tell that story.' And of course the children would remember it: he knew that.

Michael appeared to be having the time of his life, but he was thinking about the future, too. While he spent 2008 touring on the back of *Call Me Irresponsible*, he was already thinking about the next album and where he wanted to go. 'I want to take the audience with me, grow a little bit more,' he told the *Herald Sun*. 'I want to give them what it is they liked in the first place, but take it forward. I'm excited to be coming out with a new record. I know there's pressure, but I want to grow this. I'm not going to be a rapper, but at the same time I'm not going to be stuck in a box as "he sings standards".' It would be a mistake, however, to make too much of a change. Michael had, wisely, shown himself so far to be a cautious innovator. He had made his name with the classics, and although he was dipping toes in other waters, he certainly wasn't jettisoning what had made him so popular in the first place. It was a case of taking it slowly, trying out new ideas step by step.

There was also the sense of momentum to maintain. Ever since Michael had sprung into the global consciousness, he had never really been out of sight. There were times he would retreat back to his home in Vancouver, to rest between records and tours, but he was never out of the limelight for long. Now he was out there, he didn't want people to forget him, for even a moment: the world of show business is a notoriously fickle one and many an artist has broken through into the limelight, not taken full advantage of the opportunities open to them and watched their career disappear. Michael was not about to let that happen to him. He knew that he had to keep on coming out with new, accessible material and he knew he had to maintain a visible presence on the global entertainment stage. Being established was no excuse for sitting on his laurels, and Michael was smart enough to know that.

Again, there was the growing feeling that Michael was now taking charge of his whole career. He had not only enthusiasm, but authority, of a type that hadn't entirely been there before. He knew what he wanted to put on his records, and he was also a big enough name now to stand up to the record company and refuse to do exactly what they told him to if it wasn't the way he saw his own future panning out. He was daring to allow himself to think in terms of a long-term career these days, but that required strategy and planning and a sense of knowing what he was about.

He knew about the need for novelty – take Madonna, a very different artist, but one who understood that if she was to endure, she had to offer up constant new surprises. Michael might not have been in the same genre, but he was certainly aware of the need to grow if he was to survive. But he also knew he mustn't go too far in the other direction and make himself look desperate by putting out something new every five minutes. It was a fine balance that had to be struck. Give them enough to want you back – but somehow always leave them wanting more.

He elaborated on this philosophy, too. 'I have a real strong feeling that if you keep giving people the same thing they'll go, "Honey, I've got four Bublé albums, we don't need another,"' he told one interviewer. 'They wanted me to put out a whole bunch of DVDs. I don't want to do that. That's not my thing. I understand the record company needs product and that it's a business, but I'm here for a career. When something comes out I want it to last. I want my record to be on the chart for a year or two. I don't want to come out with something every few months – to me that reeks of insecurity, from the artist and the company.' Again, this showed a certain maturity, a long-term planning that might not have been obvious to everyone who'd met him in the early days. Having got what he wanted, Michael was determined to hang on to it. It had been a long haul, and he wasn't putting a strategic foot wrong now.

Michael also saw himself as something far more than just a guy who sits around making records: he was a rounded musician, with all that that implied. 'I'm not in the record business,' he said. 'This is not about CDs, this is about creating a brand name, putting on a great show so that when the next album comes out, people will be excited to hear what I've done next.' It was a very sensible and far-sighted approach, and here Michael's long apprenticeship was useful, too. He was not a kid who could be pushed around – he was a man in his thirties who'd been around a long time. It was standing him in very good stead.

He was also continually receptive to new ideas. He'd seen Blake Shelton, a country singer, cover one of his songs: why not look to the country-music industry for his own work, too? It was certainly under consideration. 'Maybe. That's more exciting to me,' Michael continued. 'I'm stockpiling songs. I'll do whatever works. I was listening to Kenny Rogers the other day. I love Kenny. The duet he does with Sheena Easton, "We've Got Tonight", is a really great song. I think Bob Seger wrote it. I listened to that and went, "Here's a really pretty song." Maybe I could do something that's a bit country. Maybe turn it into a beautiful, sexy duet that takes things on a different angle. I know people think it's cheesy, but I don't have that problem with Kenny Rogers. His version is friggin' beautiful. I was born in 1975. It's not in my memory, I have no connection to it emotionally, so when I hear it it's just raw.'

Interestingly, although he was now talking about a totally different genre of music from the one with which he is associated and with which he made his name, Michael was still emphasising that he was a modern guy, a man of his time. He'd spent years assuring people that his devotion to the classics did not mean that he was some kind of retro throwback: now he seemed to feel the need to tell everyone that he was not a country hick. Or perhaps it was the fact that it was a slightly older song, rather than a contemporary one, that was making him nervous. Either way, Michael seemed determined to make his point: he was a young guy very much of the moment, whatever the music he chose to sing.

A clue as to what his fans could expect on his next record also came through what he was performing on tour. This was a very good way of trying new numbers out and judging the audience response to them, and one interviewer picked up that Michael had been singing the great Dean Martin classic, 'You're Nobody Till Somebody Loves You'. It had been going down very well. 'That'll be on the next record, I'll produce that myself,' he said. 'I'm doing that in New York in September. I'm doing "Stardust" with [US R&B group] Naturally 7. I used to listen to this a cappella version of "Stardust" that Frank Sinatra did when I was a kid. It's so simple but dreamy.' There was certainly still a wealth of material where that came from. Michael had hardly scratched the surface of the Rat Pack music book: what with that and all the other songs he was looking at, there was the material for several dozen different albums on the horizon, with still more to spare.

Michael had now also become the subject of the various types of list people like to put together when musing about their heroes. Thus it became known that his favourite designer was Hugo Boss, his all-time favourite album was *Sinatra, Live at the Sands*, he couldn't bear to leave home without his cell phone, if he could have had any other career it would have been as a hockey player, that his favourite travel destination was Amsterdam and that his favourite way of spending his time was hanging out with the family. His dog's name is Baxter. His favourite colour is yellow. He is six feet tall. You know you've made it when people are interested in trivia about you: Michael was now well and truly in this league.

Of course, there were some rather more serious pieces of trivia out there about Michael, too. These were the snippets of information that established quite how far he'd come. For example, the record he set in 2005 at the Sydney Opera House, when one of his concerts sold the most tickets for any show at the venue ever, in one day. Or the fact that *It's Time* spent seventy-six weeks at the number one slot on the *Billboard* Top Traditional Jazz Album charts, another world record (in total, the album was on the Traditional Jazz Album and Current Jazz Album charts for 101 weeks). Or that 'Home' was the most heard song on Canadian radio in 2005. It is believed 382 million people heard it.

That was really where Michael was now and in September 2008, it was announced that he was to grace the front cover of *Chatelaine*, a woman's lifestyle and interest magazine, only the third man ever to do so after the former Prime Minister Pierre Trudeau and the hockey player Wayne Gretzky. 'And the first cross dresser,' added Michael brightly, when he was interviewed about the announcement. But, joking aside, he was clearly extremely pleased. 'It's a huge honour and to be in that company is pretty amazing,' he said. 'I was thrilled when they asked me to do it.'

So was he as great a character as the other two? 'That or my hair,' said Michael. 'Maybe they think I have good hair.' Becoming more serious, he continued, 'I don't know that it's meant to be put in that perspective. I don't think it should be. I don't see myself as someone who's as important as Trudeau or as prolific as Wayne Gretzky.' He did, however, say give it another twenty years – yet another clear sign that he was letting himself think ahead, career-wise.

Oh, and was he a regular reader of *Chatelaine*? Er – 'I'm not a big magazine guy,' Michael replied.

It was now that the split with Emily had happened, and for all his larking around on other topics, Michael was clearly finding this a sensitive one. But he was staying schtumm. 'There will be nothing to take away her dignity or to give away secrets that would make her uncomfortable or make her feel exposed,' he said. 'Or any of the women that I've ever been with. How does anyone feel when they break up out of a long relationship? It's tough. It's shit. It hurts. You're sentimental. You wish you'd done things differently.' It was a brave stance, but in this case, Michael just could not avoid looking vulnerable. This was a very wounding episode for him. The scars continued to appear raw.

Emily has also remained silent, although she has made what could have been taken as the odd pointed remark. When the film *The Young Victoria*, in which she played the title role, premiered, she took as her perfect man Queen Victoria's consort, Prince Albert. 'This is what I look for in a man,' she said. 'He's my definition of a real man, because he encouraged her in a very selfless way, to be the best version of herself she could possibly be.' On Michael, or any possible successor, she refused to be drawn. Indeed, it seemed that she had learned a few lessons herself over the last few years, about what was wise to talk about and what was not. 'If you openly talk about your relationship, when things go south – which they did – what you've said is still very much in the public domain, when you don't want it to be any longer,' is all she would say. Whatever the reality of what had gone on, it was clear the two of them had both been bruised.

On a rather cheerier note, Michael was also becoming rather preoccupied with the fact that the 2010 winter Olympics were to be held in Vancouver, something that he as a British Columbian was getting very worked up about. Would he be singing at the ceremony? 'I've not been approached,' said Michael. 'I would hope to see some BC [British Columbian] people: myself or Diana [Krall] or Sarah McLachlan. I'm proud of this place and I was thrilled when we got it. I'm looking forward to it. If I'm not invited, I'll be there watching. Honestly. Who needs the pressure? As much as it's an honour, if you don't get invited, you don't get invited. What are you going to do?' And what, he was asked, would happen if someone like Bryan Adams or McLachlan was asked to take part and he wasn't? 'Then heads would roll,' said Michael. 'Me and Nelly Furtado would sit and come up with a plan of revenge.' The Bublé humour was there, as strong as ever: there was certainly none of the griping in the way there had been about the Grammys. Michael had learned his lesson there.

The photo shoot went ahead and in the event, when *Chatelaine* came out it was a huge success. Michael used the occasion to reveal his five favourite love songs: 'Take a Look At Me Now' by Phil Collins, 'God Only Knows' by the

Beach Boys, 'Crying' by Roy Orbison, 'At This Moment' by Billy Vera and the Beaters and 'You Don't Know Me' by Ray Charles. Shortly afterwards, he got pretty much the ultimate endorsement from Michael Parkinson: 'This young man, I think he has got the lot,' Parkinson declared. 'He's got the looks, the style, and of course, the voice. He has the ability to tell the story and the lyric. Bublé's version of the classic song "The Way You Look Tonight" is better than Frank Sinatra's. I can think of no greater praise than that.'

Nor indeed could anyone else. Coming from Parky, that was the equivalent of the young pretender finally being crowned king. If probably the most influential arbiter of taste in Britain, the home of so much great music and, indeed, to so many of Michael's fans, called him the best, then who could gainsay that? Certainly the quibbles about his copying other vocalists were long gone: Michael was now standing head and shoulders above most of the crowd. All that early potential had been more than fulfilled.

Towards the end of the year, it was announced that *Call Me Irresponsible* was at number one on the *Billboard* chart again, the sixty-fifth time it had been so since its release. It was proving to be as popular as its predecessor – Michael had done it again. But he still refused to sit on his laurels: Michael was about to set out to tour again, this time to South America, where he'd never been before.

Michael's charity work was also of increasing importance to him. More of the great and good causes came his way: now Michael became an ambassador for British Columbia Children's Hospital Foundation's Campaign for BC Children. The foundation was trying to raise money to build a new children's hospital. 'For me, helping BC was a very simple choice,' said Michael. 'My cousins have been to BC Children's

Hospital, as have I when I was little. Whatever I can do to help, I will do it.'

The hospital itself was clearly delighted. 'We are privileged to have Michael Bublé on our team,' said Don Lindsay, chair of the campaign. 'Michael is remarkably talented, he has a great way with people, and clearly has a deep commitment to BC's communities.' He did, but more than that, he was not just a celebrity – he was someone who could make a difference. That meant more than anything.

He was to prove similarly generous in February 2009, when terrible bush fires swept across the southeastern Australian state of Victoria. The country had always been deeply welcoming to Michael and now he returned the favour: he was one of a number of international stars who joined forces to raise money for the Red Cross. Nicole Kidman and Keith Urban, an Australian couple themselves, led the way, donating AUS\$500,000, backed up by the likes of Russell Crowe, Hugh Jackman, Naomi Watts and many more. Michael donated AUS\$50,000: a way of saying thank you, perhaps, to a country that had given him a great deal, and a way of trying to help now that it was in distress.

Indeed, Michael was displaying an increasingly strong philanthropic streak as time wore on. The list of charities he'd done work for was growing: as well as Hear the World, it now included the Celebrity Fight Night Foundation, 21st Century Leaders, Charity Projects Entertainment Fund, Keep Memory Alive, the Muhammad Ali Parkinson Center, MusiCan and Whatever It Takes. He got back quite as much as he gave: the satisfaction of knowing that he was helping the vulnerable in society, and in some ways repaying a world that had given him so much.

With some celebrities who espouse charitable causes, there

is the sense that they merely feel the need to go through the motions. That could not have been further from the case with Michael. He came from a humble background, he knew what it was like to have to struggle. Even though in the case of his background, it was money the family had to worry about and not ill health, the point was that he knew what life could be like when it wasn't running smoothly, and he genuinely wanted to use his celebrity to help others. With Michael, what you saw was well and truly what you got.

12

Michael Bublé, Vancouver Giant

It was December 2008. Michael Bublé, world-class superstar, had just had one of the greatest honours bestowed upon him in his life. This was not another musical award or yet another platinum album, however – it was a minority stake in the Vancouver Giants, the city's famous ice-hockey team. 'I've done lots of amazing things in my life, but this is easily the most prestigious for me,' said Michael, as he was presented with his own team jersey. 'It's a dream come true to be a part of this club. It [ice hockey] is a huge part of my life, and I'm sentimental about it, actually. It's part of our life, it's almost the soundtrack to our life, especially here in Vancouver. My plans are honestly to watch these boys. As long as they don't tell me what songs to put on my record, I promise I ain't gonna tell them who to put on the ice.'

It was a wise move. There was no doubting Michael's commitment to the team and the game, but there were naysayers about the place who were of the opinion that a crooner had no business owning an ice-hockey team, or even a part of one. Was Michael not an entertainer who made women swoon? How could that possibly have any part in the macho world of men's ice hockey?

That was not, however, a view that prevailed across the board. Michael had by now become something of an ambassador for his native Vancouver, not least because of the growing amount of charity work he did, and as a member of the great and good, he was the ideal person to be a part owner of the city's ice-hockey team. There were several other well-known minority owners, including Sultan Thiara, former Toronto Maple Leafs and Vancouver Canucks coach, Pat Quinn, and National Hockey League legend, Gordie Howe.

But an ice-hockey team, Michael's beloved game . . . Never in his wildest dreams would he have been able to see this coming all those years ago as he was slogging around the nightclub circuit, desperate for the break that it seemed would never come. This was something else. To own a nice house was one thing, but an ice-hockey team? If ever Michael needed assurance that he had made it, this was it. This was the ultimate toy (not that Michael would ever have dreamed of describing it as such), the ultimate status symbol, the ultimate example of quite how far he had come in the world. Where were the regular guys who thought he was a dork way back in school? Where were all the disparagers who'd made fun of the music and never thought Michael would amount to anything? He was now sewn into the heart of Vancouver, all the more so because of his association with the Giants, a symbol of his city, his country and its glorious game. He was in a different league now, not a star or even a superstar, but someone enmeshed indelibly with the public consciousness. He was in the foremost ranks of famous Canadians. Around the world, people who had never even heard of Vancouver or the Vancouver Giants had heard of Michael Bublé.

The majority owner, Ron Toigo, was extremely enthusiastic about Michael's involvement. 'It's all about doing the right thing . . . and being involved in something that has a chance to win,' he said. 'The Giants is a brand, and Michael certainly brings awareness to the brand.' And on the subject of his music, he certainly didn't see a problem. 'I think Michael's music is very versatile,' he said. 'There's iPods with Metallica to Bublé. I think people are more versatile in what they listen to nowadays, and it's obvious because he sells right across the board.'

If truth be told, Michael was beside himself with happiness at the turn of events. This was more than a dream come true: this was an introduction into one of the most exclusive clubs in the world. 'I couldn't be more thrilled to be a part of such a wonderful team, management and ownership – a group of winners!' he said. 'It's a dream come true to be a part of this club, I can't believe it's happened. I talked to Jim Balsillie [a passionate hockey fan, who was also co-chief executive of the company that developed the Blackberry] a couple of days ago and it's probably the first and only time he'll be jealous of me.'

Indeed, given the strength and depth of Michael's interest, it was surprising he was managing to sound as calm as he did. If ever there was a case of handing a child the key to the cookie cupboard, this was it. 'My goal, and it might be a ridiculously silly goal, is that I would love to own the Canucks one day as well,' he said. 'I have a lot of work to do but, you know, you dream, right? You set 'em high and if you don't make it, you still land pretty close to where you want. This is a huge start for me.'

Indeed, Michael's passion for ice hockey was only secondary to his passion for music. 'If you ask my dad and my mom, my hockey career started in our house and garage where I ruined every wall because I put hockey pucks through them,' said Michael. 'I played as a kid and I think my hands were pretty good but my skating was atrocious. I watched Pavel Bure and I figured if he can wait at the [red] line, I can do that, too. But apparently I wasn't as fast as Pavel. I went to every single home game as a kid and I remember those beautiful yellow jerseys that everyone thought were so ugly.'

Michael was becoming very nearly poetic by now. As well as summing up to him his country, ice hockey had always been a part of his life. It brought back his earliest childhood memories; it had been a constant ever since he could remember. This really was a consolidation of everything he had ever done.

'I remember I wanted to be Gary Lupul, I wanted to be Patrik Sundstrom and Ivan Hlinka,' Michael continued, on his way down nostalgia road. 'I used to think that being named Michael Bublé was pretty cool because I was close to being called Jiri Bubla. I'm yelled at by all my British friends who tell me their football is a real sport and my American friends that their kind of football is a real sport but I don't know. Hockey to me is the fastest, most beautiful, intricate game there is. I love it. I love playing it, I love watching it, I eat it, I drink it. A couple of nights ago, me and a few friends were having a few beers and they asked me what I couldn't live without and when I thought about it, sadly, I think I could live without music but I don't think I could live without hockey. I think it's the greatest game on Earth.'

That was pretty obvious. Much has been made of Michael's boyishness: his new plaything was bringing that side of his nature out to the full. 'If I'm at home, I'll show up at the games and, if I'm on tour, I'll watch them on TV or the computer,' he continued. 'I think they've created an amazing culture of winning from ownership to management to the coaching staff and players. Their drafting, their trading, I mean everything they've done has been right on.' He might almost have been talking about himself. But this was his reward: the sign of what he had achieved. By now, Michael was as much a Vancouver Giant as anyone on the team that he now partly owned.

In January 2009, Michael took part in another experiment that made something of a splash, a documentary on CTV Canada called *The Musical Brain*. Sting, Wyclef Jean and Leslie Feist also took part: the documentary was set to illustrate how the brain uses music to shape the human experience. It taught him a great deal about himself.

'I learned that what I was insecure about – me thinking that I wasn't as brilliant as some other writer because I write [with my emotions] – it actually was really nice to learn that most human beings have responded the same way as I do to music,' Michael explained. 'So I'm more the norm when it comes down to it.'

Sting, on the other hand, was nothing like as comfortable discussing the subject matter, eventually saying he didn't enjoy examining the science behind the music. 'He writes in a completely different way,' said Michael. 'They said at one point in the special that he almost gets the same kind of emotional kick out of playing Sudoku that he does writing. For me, it's purely emotional. So, I never really have had to second-guess myself too much because, emotionally, I'm pretty honest with myself. I know what I like and what I don't.'

Michael's reactions to the experiment brought out more

than just his attitude towards his own insecurities: they also proved once and for all that he was quite as talented when it came to writing music as he was at singing it. The full depth of his talent was coming out now, the full range of what he was able to do. And his pleasure in performing was obvious: the sheer delight he took in the music he was able to make and what it meant to him was immensely engaging to anyone observing from the side.

'A chord makes me feel a certain thing,' Michael continued. 'A lyric matched perfectly with that chord helps me to decipher what I think is a hit song. When someone tells you that your brain is working like most of the world's . . . it tells you that if you think a song is a hit, that you have a good chance that it will be. And maybe other people will respond the same way to what makes you hot about it.'

Michael was contributing to other shows at this point, too, another being *30 Rock*, starring Alec Baldwin. He recorded a song called 'Mr Templeton' for the show, in which Baldwin's character went out with a nurse played by Salma Hayek. Hayek had previously gone through Baldwin's record collection, teasing him, 'I didn't know Michael Bublé had so many albums.'

Michael was rather chuffed about it all. 'I kept getting phone calls and emails from people saying, "Man, they're talking about you on the show the last couple weeks,"' he said. Alec and Salma then both asked that Michael write a song especially for the show. He duly obliged.

There were plenty of other television appearances, too: he made a cameo appearance on the 100th landmark episode of the Canadian show *Corner Gas* in an episode entitled 'TV Free Dog River': Senior Officer Davis turned the Dog River police station into such a good all-jazz station that even

Michael couldn't get airplay. It was very good natured stuff. He also put in an appearance on *The Chris Isaak Hour* on the Bio Channel. The programme was designed to allow artists to tell their stories through their music. If there was anyone for whom this was suitable, it was Michael Bublé.

He still couldn't, though, despite everything, believe that such famous people actually knew who he was. He'd known Salma Hayek was a fan – a 'really nice, beautiful woman', according to Michael, but even so. That someone as famous as Salma appreciated him – 'It's always nice to hear that,' he said. 'I live in Vancouver, and I'm not a big celeb guy who goes to red carpets, so it's always a surprise when someone you admire likes what you do.'

Meanwhile, work was going on behind the scenes. Michael started work on a new original track, 'I Just Haven't Met You Yet': at the time of writing, his next CD was under way, but had not yet been named. 'He's working hard on the new disc as he wants it to be, in his words, "Fabulous" – the process of recording the kind of music that Michael loves takes a great deal of time – and they typically start with a huge list of songs and trim it down to ones they are certain will work on an album and also when he performs them live,' said a spokesperson. 'He always jokes that they've got to be songs he loves 'cause he'll sing them every night for the next two years.'

And he continued in his role among the great and good. Michael was one of the many stars present when Leeza Gibbons and Olivia Newton John got together with David Foster for the first Leeza Gibbons 'Night To Make a Difference', which took place at the famous Mr Chow restaurant in Beverly Hills. Michael made an impromptu performance on the night, much to the delight of the assembled guests.

He was also thoroughly enjoying everything that went with

his status as part-owner of the Vancouver Giants. He went on the Vancouver sports station Team 1040 as a colour commentator, filling in for Tom Larscheid, the regular analyst. This really was the vindication of all that had gone before: his great love, music, had allowed him to become immersed in his other great love, ice hockey. The wheel had turned full circle: Michael's life was complete.

Quite how far Michael had come became apparent in March 2009, when it was announced that he was to be inducted into the British Columbia Entertainment Hall of Fame for 2009. His name was to be embedded in a sidewalk along Vancouver's Granville Street Entertainment Row: it was an honour doled out to British Columbians who had made an outstanding contribution to the entertainment industry, locally, in Canada and abroad. Michael had certainly done that. And this was more than just record sales, gratifying though they were, and sold-out tours, which were more gratifying still: this was recognition from his country and his peers for what he had achieved. If he hadn't previously realised the full scale of what he'd done, he certainly did now.

So where next? Still a relatively young man, Michael Bublé looks to have a long career ahead. He is worth millions and need never work again, but that, as for any committed performer, is not the point. Frank Sinatra, to whom he is so often compared, never really gave up touring until he became too ill to carry on, although he stopped needing to do so for the money approximately five decades earlier. Michael looks set to emulate the great man there, too.

But whether by luck or judgement, or a combination of the two, Michael has made some decisions that will stand him in very good stead for a lengthy career. For a start, he writes his own music, or at least some of it, and all those cover versions, the songs he wrote himself sung by different people, are going to bring him royalties. This is far and away the best way of building up a fortune in the music industry. Secondly, he has started to produce his own material. Both of these aspects to his career mean that should the public ever tire of Michael Bublé's music, then there's still plenty of scope to do a huge amount of work with other artists.

There's also the possibility of acting, something Michael did, after all, dabble in at the start of his career. He appears to have ruled it out for the moment, but that is not to say it won't rear its head again in the future. His popularity is such that fans are bound to support any projects he becomes involved with: it may yet make a reappearance in the Bublé repertoire.

As for romance . . . At the time of writing, there has been no replacement for Emily Blunt. There is no question that Michael wants to be a husband and father – that, after all, was the reason he nearly gave up at the beginning of it all – but paradoxically, the more wealthy, famous and thus eligible he becomes, the more difficult it is to meet the right kind of woman. He is a target, these days, for women who want a career off the back of their association with him, or just to be with someone rich and famous. But that is not what Michael himself wants from a prospective partner: he wants someone who will want him for who he really is. And there is no sign of any let-up in the touring schedule either, which will also make it difficult to create the time to nurture a relationship. On top of that, there are some fairly strong signs he is not yet over Emily. It could be a while before he settles down.

So what, then, has been the real secret of his success? Charm, charisma, talent and a glint in his eye all play a part. But Michael's story is also one of an immigrant family who, by dint of hard work, makes a life and a career on foreign shores. Then the younger generation comes along and, with all the vast potential that that amazing continent has to offer those who are prepared to work for it, goes on to have a career that the older generation couldn't have even dreamt about. It happened to Frank Sinatra, another singer from an Italian background, and it happened to Michael, too.

'My story has been pretty neat,' is how Michael himself put it. 'To be honest with you, I grew up in a wonderful place in a wonderful country. My family gave me unconditional love as I grew up. Middle-class, work hard, blue-collar family. I have never had anything terrible happen in my life. God blessed me with having a healthy family and good people around me. I feel in love with this music. Besides the fact of being discovered by the Prime Minister, David Foster and Paul Anka, the story is not all that exciting. I wish there was a little bit more drama.' It was a fairly modest appraisal of what was turning out to be quite a life.

But perhaps the most important person in this story apart from Michael himself is his beloved Grandpa Mitch, still watching every step of his increasingly famous grandson's career with great joy. It was Mitch who gave him the music bug, Mitch who encouraged him to sing in the first place, Mitch who paid for his singing lessons, Mitch who installed plumbing for free so that nightclub owners would give his grandson a turn on stage, Mitch who stood behind him and urged him not to quit when times were tough and Mitch who has been enjoying Michael's astonishing success very nearly as much as Michael himself.

'Learn it before I die . . .' – has ever the request from grand-father to grandson produced such results before? Sunshine most certainly had the talent, but what he has also had every step along the way is someone who believes in him. Small wonder that with Mitch on his side, he went on to conquer the music industry around the globe. Small wonder that his career took off in the way it did. And what a testament to Michael that he has shared his happiness and his success with Mitch and the rest of his family every step along the way.

And, perhaps most importantly of all, Michael has spread a great deal of happiness with what he does. Whether it's just by keeping the old songs alive or putting on a belter of a performance, Michael is a world-famous pop star, loved by all generations and, whisper it, with fans among men as well as women, too. He came, he saw, he entertained. As he himself might put it – let the good times roll.

Index